Fuchs, Lawrence H.

The political behavior of
American Jews

DATE DUE			

The Political Behavior of
American Jews

The Political Behavior
of
American Jews

By

LAWRENCE H. FUCHS

Assistant Professor of Political Science, Brandeis University

GREENWOOD PRESS, PUBLISHERS
WESTPORT, CONNECTICUT

Library of Congress Cataloging in Publication Data

Fuchs, Lawrence H
    The political behavior of American Jews.

    Reprint of the ed. published by Free Press,
Glencoe, Ill.
    Includes bibliographical references and index.
    1. Jews in the United States--Politics and govern-
ment. 2. Party affiliation--United States. 3. United
States--Politics and government. I. Title.
[E184.J5F8 1980]   323.1'1924'073   79-28711
ISBN 0-313-22282-7 lib. bdg.

Reprinted with the permission of The Free Press, A Division of
Macmillan Publishing Co., Inc.

Reprinted in 1980 by Greenwood Press, a division of Congressional
Information Service, Inc., 51 Riverside Avenue, Westport
Connecticut 06880

Printed in the United States of America

10 9 8 7 6 5 4 3 2 1

Preface

THERE ARE many reasons for writing a book. I wrote this one primarily because the subject interested me and I wanted to find out more about it. I still want to find out more about it, and if any reader cares to pass along comments or information which will shed further light on the analysis I have attempted, his correspondence will be gratefully received.

I know that both the anti-Semite and the philo-Semite will find material here which they can put to their own uses. My earnest hope and belief is that the vast majority of readers will receive the book in the same spirit of honest inquiry with which I tried to write it. Since I believe in the basic unity of man, I would be greatly disturbed to know that anyone used material from this book to argue that the Jews are "better" or "worse" than any other group. That they are different is clear, and that cultural differences are a proper subject for study in the social sciences should also be clear.

There are acknowledgments to make to many people, none of whom ought to share the slightest blame for the errors and blemishes which may appear in the following pages. I owe debts of gratitude to: Rupert Emerson, who was Chairman of the Government Department at Harvard when I began work on this book, and who gave me much encouragement; Dr. Eleanor Maccoby and Professor Frederick Mosteller for the help they gave me in preparing my research design for the survey; Professor Gordon Allport for his encouragement and his ideas on questionnaire design for the survey; Sol Kolak, the Director of the Boston Office of the Anti-Defamation League of B'nai B'rith for his interest; the administrators of the Sigmund Livingston Fund of the

Anti-Defamation League for a grant of funds to conclude the Boston survey; the librarians at Widener Library and Brandeis University, who were ever gracious and helpful; my own students at Brandeis in my course in Political Parties for letting me use them as a sounding-board; those students at Brandeis who volunteered to help me conduct a pilot project; my colleagues Kenneth Olson of Harvard, Richard Ekaus of Brandeis, and Victor Fuchs of Columbia for their constructive suggestions and criticisms; Miss Lisa Rosenfarb, a student at Radcliffe, who helped me conduct and code interviews; Brandeis students Judith Bleich, Sheila Ekaus, Cynthia Rich, and Gail Rubenstein for their statistical compilations and other help; and to my wife, who was a faithful proofreader and critic, and who, along with our two daughters, put up with much nonsense from me while this book gestated.

A special word of thanks must go to Professor V. O. Key of Harvard, who read the entire manuscript in several versions. The queries he raised invariably pointed up deficiencies of my own and suggested fruitful ways of handling my material.

To my mother, who died when I was finishing research for this study, and to whom I owe more than words can say, I dedicate this book.

LAWRENCE H. FUCHS

Cambridge, Mass.

Contents

(7)

Contents   (9)

Tables

Foreword

THE QUESTION of the place of the church poses a perplexing problem for the architects of political systems. The American solution of separation of church and state rests on the incontestable lesson of history that the clerics, once they capture power in the state, have a formidable capacity to restrict the liberties of the citizen and to oppress the unbelievers and the dissidents, often most cruelly and always in the name of God. Yet the inscription of the constitutional doctrine on parchment does not set up a dike between religion and politics, which are almost inevitably intertwined. The practical problem of the maintenance of religious liberty and the prevention of religious excesses consists in the development of habits of tolerance and of restraint in the day-to-day actions of men. In this endeavor the United States has achieved a considerable success. Our occasional mass outbursts of intolerance and our scattered instances of clerical abuse of political power are insignificant alongside the astonishing fact that the most diverse sorts of believers have managed to live together relatively peaceably for a long period of time.

In this book Professor Fuchs explores the place of the Jews in our pluralistic equilibrium among ethno-religious groups. The unmolested existence of the Jews in America, in contrast with their difficulties in many other parts of the world, represents, of course, a striking illustration of the workings of our system of religious freedom. In turn, the contribution of the Jews to our political life neatly exemplifies the process by which the many cultural strands that make up America are somehow woven together into an operating political order even though each may retain to a considerable extent its own integrity. Professor Fuchs describes the role of the Jews in American politics and seeks out the whys of that role. Although there may be dissent from some of his explanations of the whys, the record he presents scarcely permits dissent from the proposition that the Jews have served the Republic well.

While Professor Fuchs' account will have an appeal to all those with a curiosity about the great game of politics, students of politics will find of special interest the manner in which the questions raised in the book are attacked. Since he has fallen prey to no methodological monomania, Professor Fuchs has been free to employ an ingenious combination of techniques and approaches as well as a wide variety of types of data in developing his analysis.

V. O. KEY, JR.

Cambridge, Massachusetts
September 5, 1955

CHAPTER I

"But Is There A Jewish Vote?"

THE STUDY of politics rests largely upon an analysis of group interest and its expression. One type of group which the students and practitioners of politics have long recognized as worthy of attention is the ethno-religious group.[1] Politicians, in the quest for votes, have recognized the persistence of ethno-religious loyalties by balancing slates, planning campaigns, and seeking out issues in order to assuage the grievances or promote the causes of some ethno-religious group. Political writers have produced a plethora of literature on foreign and immigrant influences in American politics.

Yet, there persists a curious disbelief that religion or national origin have anything to do with the way a judge makes up his mind in a case involving social policy, or the way a government executive administers a law, or the way an ordinary citizen votes. The question I am most often asked by persons interested in the subject of this book is, "But is there a Jewish vote?" The answer depends, of course, on what the questioner means. If he or she means, do all Jews

---

1. The term "ethno-religious" is used because of its inclusive quality. By using the term "ethno-religious" I mean to include ethnic groups such as the Italians, religious groups such as the Quakers, and ethno-religious groups such as the Irish-Catholics or the Jews. Color minorities such as the Negroes are included. I have accepted Robin Williams definition of an ethnic group as "one possessing continuity through biological descent whose members share a distinctive social and cultural tradition." (*The Reduction of Intergroup Tensions* [New York: Social Science Research Council], 1947, p. 42.)

react the same way to candidates and issues, then the answer is obviously no. If the query simply means, does being Jewish sometimes influence one's political attitudes and behavior, then the answer is, certainly. In this sense there is not only a Jewish vote but an Irish, Polish, Armenian, and even a Baptist and Episcopalian vote.

There is no automatic formula for showing how being Jewish affects political behavior any more than there is one for showing how being an Episcopalian shapes political attitudes. One group may show a high degree of political unity in one place at a certain time—such as the Episcopalians in Connecticut in the election of 1811, when they voted as a block to protest against the distribution of funds between their Bishop's Fund and Yale College. Another group may be sharply divided on a major political question, such as the Methodists in their approach to the issue of prohibition.

"Will Jews vote for a Jew?" is another question that is always asked during a discussion of this subject. The answer is that sometimes they will and sometimes they will not, depending on a wide range of factors. Individual reactions to Jewish names on the ballot will vary from the chauvinistic response of a seventy-year-old housewife I interviewed in Dorchester who told me that she voted for Jewish names regardless of party, to the peculiar attitude of one young high-school teacher who said he always tried to vote for one non-Jewish candidate regardless of merit, to prove his broadmindedness.

Jews are no different than others in this respect. Americans are not divided by classical political issues. It is the hoopla and acrobatics of politics which absorb their interest. The political philosophies of contesting parties and candidates often seem quite similar. When issues and party philosophies are not important to voters, they look to the personal qualifications of candidates. Such things as attendance at the right church may become important to them, and if all other things appear to be equal, they will vote for their own kind.

Ignorance of or indifference to the issues also promotes "name" voting. Ignorance of the issues or the nonexistence of exciting issues is especially prevalent in state and local contests. Without issues to guide them, voters get their bearings from party affiliations and their knowledge of the personality characteristics of the candidates. But party affiliation is not likely to mean a great deal to most voters when it comes to such matters as the laying of a sewer pipe and zoning regulations. And the growth of nonpartisan primaries and elections or city-wide proportional representation elections de-emphasize even more the relationship of party affiliation to local politics. Confronted with long ballots and frequent elections, a great many voters rely upon the recognition of familiar-sounding names in order to make their choices. One sheriff or dog catcher is presumably as good as another. Should an Italian be expected to vote for a Polish Registrar of Deeds when a Fischetti is in the field?

There are times when other factors will control the vote. In 1922 when the Jewish Tammany leader, Henry Frank, candidate for Congress from New York City's 20th Congressional District, charged his opponent, Fiorello LaGuardia, with anti-Semitism, the charge actually backfired. Most Jews in the district knew LaGuardia too well to be taken in by Frank's tactics, and the pint-sized Italian won in the Jewish district by a substantial plurality.

The complete block voting of ethnic groups is virtually a thing of the past except perhaps in Duval, Starr, and Webb counties in Southern Texas where boss George Parr, through his Mexican intermediaries, has in recent years been able to organize and deliver over ninety per cent of the Mexican vote to any candidate he designates. But in the 1830's and 1840's the German and Irish vote in New York City could often be delivered in a block. The members of immigrant groups have always been particularly responsive to direction and leadership from within their own group by those supposed to be in the know. Lacking information and experience in American politics, often unable to speak English, distrustful of outsiders, immigrants gave special weight to advice given them by one of their own kind in their own language. Oftentimes votes were returned for friendly acts— help with the immigration officials and with citizenship papers, or getting a job or a place to live. It was little enough payment to accept the political advice of more experienced "landsmen" who had befriended them. Politics was too remote from their experience and at the same time too difficult to understand. Lithuanian clubs in Chicago or Polish clubs in Detroit still play an important role in party politics, but many groups such as the Dutch, the Scandinavians, and the Jews themselves are highly individualistic in politics.

There exists in this country a widespread feeling that religion and national origin should play no part in determining political opinions. Most Americans seem to feel that ethno-religious influences in politics are somehow "un-American." I have even encountered audiences who felt that talking about such influences was a bad thing. One ought to vote as an American and not as an Irish-American or Jewish-American, is the commonly expressed attitude. But students of politics know that voting decisions are the products of many group influences. Yet no one says that one ought to vote as an American and not as a farmer-American or a businessman-American. The very phrases sound absurd.

The suspicion that ethno-religious influences in politics might be detrimental to American democracy or the national welfare is not without foundation. Ethno-religious politics sometimes manifests itself in ways that seem clearly dangerous. There has always been considerable tension in this country between whites and Negroes, between old and new immigrant groups, and among religious groups. The attempts of politicians to feed on this tension and even manufacture more of it are obviously deplorable. Few would quarrel with the quest of ethnic and religious groups to win representation in various governmental positions. But the deliberate attempts of politicians to drum up fears, recall old enmities, and reopen wounds in the scramble for votes makes it more difficult to work out a harmonious solution to pluralism in America. The spectre of Negro hegemony over South Carolina, Catholic or Jewish rule in Washington, or British control of Boston and Chicago have often been cast before the eyes of Americans at election time. Such appeals can be even more dangerous than class appeals, because they are much more precise, and the objects of hostility, living clustered in a single neighborhood, can often be identified by physical characteristics.

There is still another reason why apprehension is justified when ethnic and religious factors become important determinants of public policy. The kinds of issues which induce ethnic or religious unity at the polls are explosive precisely because feelings about them are so intense. These matters may infringe on the private manners, morals, and customs of different groups. Such questions as the prohibition of alcohol for drinking, permissible types of religious activity, gambling, and birth control are often subject to public policy at the state and local level. What makes these issues more corrosive socially than farm parity or labor management questions is that they raise the problem of the delicate relationship of church and state. Protestants and Jews do not like to be told that they cannot purchase contraceptives, any more than Catholics want to be prevented from sending their children to parochial schools because of the absence of public transportation.

A third factor which justifies the concern which many Americans share when ethno-religious influences play a large role in shaping public policy has to do with foreign policy. Millions of voters, or their immediate forebears, emigrated from nations which are constantly engaged in intercourse with the United States. The fact that there are more than five million foreign-born citizens in eight pivotal states with 213 electoral votes in Presidential elections, makes foreign policy acutely subject to the feelings of various ethnic groups. From the stormy political controversy over the Jay Treaty with the British in 1794, which provoked the mass opposition of Irishmen, to the Polish denunciations of the Yalta agreement in recent Presidential elections, the hyphenated groups have not been shy about trying to shape American foreign policy. The Irish appear to have been particularly sensitive to foreign entanglements because, since the administration of James Monroe, American foreign policy has been based largely on friendship for Great Britain. For example, Irish activity played a major role in defeating a fisheries treaty with Canada in 1888 and the general Anglo-American Arbitration Treaty in 1897. Other groups—the Germans, Italians, Dutch, and Jews—have urged particular foreign policies on the nation from time to time. German-Americans attempted to get the United States to settle a dispute between the homeland, England, and this country over the Pacific island of Samoa in a way favorable to Germany in 1888. At the turn of the century Hollanders tried to get the United States to intervene in the Boer war. Ethnic and even religious feelings are still vital factors in the determination of public attitudes on foreign policy. Nonintervention in the Spanish Civil War was, to some extent, forced on the United States by Catholic opinion. The howls of protest with which Protestant groups met President Truman's decision to appoint an Ambassador to the Vatican made him reverse his action. American Jews are partisans of Israel, and were instrumental in having the United States become the first government to recognize the infant republic.

Why is it more dangerous for Polish-Americans to try to change foreign policy than for the American Medical Association to make national health policy? Both groups may advance programs which are inimical to the national welfare. The fact is that foreign policy is and should be much more a matter of expertise than most domestic questions. Also, jeopardizing the national interest in foreign policy is likely to be a much more dangerous matter than hurting the commonweal in domestic affairs. One of the difficulties, or, from the point of view of democracy, one of the advantages is that no one really knows what the general welfare will be in the long run. The late Secretary of Defense, James Forrestal, with one eye on America's diminishing oil reserves, suffered anguish over the activity of American Zionists. The politicians in both parties, he thought, were sacrificing the national interest in the Middle East for a mess of Jewish votes. As it turned out, American national interest is probably better served by the establishment of the democratic state of Israel than it would have been if Arab nations had been placated. Although the experts are sometimes wrong and the special pleaders right, it still ought to be presumed that the former will usually be better able to interpret American interests abroad than the latter.

While it is sensible to realize that there are dangers in ethno-religious politics, it would be ridiculous to ignore its existence and even more silly to implore its cessation. Ethno-religious politics is basically a product of ethno-religious pluralism in American life. It is harmless to exhort citizens to vote in the national interest and not in behalf of their group interests, but it is also ineffective. Rarely do voters perceive any clear-cut conflict between the national interest and the group interests which they espouse. Bankers usually urge a hard money policy not for the benefit of bankers, but for the good of the national economy. Labor leaders offer explanations for the closed shop in terms of the public welfare. Lithuanians demand the liberation of the Soviet satellites in order to defend American concepts of justice and freedom. Most of us either equate our group interests with the general welfare or never think of the general welfare at all.

Unless one clearly perceives a conflict between the national welfare and the interests of his own special group he ought not to be ashamed of voting to influence policy in favor of his ethnic group, any more than he would be unhappy about voting to influence policy in favor of his occupational group. Such a clear conflict of interests is unlikely. Quakers who advocate pacifism hardly think they are working against the national interest any more than Ukranians who wish to invade the Soviet Union as soon as possible. Moreover, group expression in politics is indispensable to democracy. It would be undemocratic as well as impossible to silence some groups and permit others to speak out.

Americans are still overly nervous about the phenomenon of ethnic and religious influences in politics even though considerable progress has been made in recent decades and despite the legitimate reasons for apprehension. The fact that one's Jewishness influences his politics is not necessarily any less American than if one's class interest or occupational interest determines his politics. In fact, a strong case can be made that ethno-religious diversity in American society has been a major factor in mitigating class cleavage. Whether that is a good or bad thing depends somewhat on your view of the American refusal to see politics wholly in class terms. At least it can be argued that a love of one's God or of the culture of the old country are as healthy influences on American politics as a crass involvement in a trade association or a labor union.

Jews, being a particularly sensitive minority, have always been afraid to admit that a Jew's politics might be affected by his religion. Acute concern over allegations of a Jewish vote have led Hebrew publicists into absurd positions. In 1928 in New York State an editorial writer for the *American Hebrew* sounded a note of warning lest the Republican candidate for Governor, Albert Ottinger, and the Democratic candidate for Lieutenant Governor, Herbert Lehman, be elected simultaneously as a result of Jewish ticket-splitting. As it turned out the Jewish districts preferred Ottinger's opponent, Franklin Roosevelt. But what if Ottinger and Lehman had clearly been the best men in the field? Should Jewish voters purposely have voted against one of the best men to escape the charge of a Jewish vote? Similarly, spokesmen for the Democratic Party in 1904 and the Republican National Committee in 1940 warned Jews against voting for Theodore Roosevelt in the first instance and Franklin Roosevelt in the second because of claims which would follow of a

Jewish vote. But most Jews were persuaded that the first Roosevelt in 1904 and F.D.R. in 1940 were especially understanding friends of the Jewish people. Should they have rewarded that friendship by voting for their opponents? The question is academic, of course. The vast majority of Jews voted for both Roosevelts.

No one in his right mind will argue that a Jew ought to vote for a Jew when he knows his coreligionist is clearly the inferior man, or that an Irishman ought to call for a policy which he knows is bad for the rest of his countrymen. But the time for nervousness about ethno-religious politics is over. When assertions are made that American Jews helped to formulate American policy in the Middle East, leaders ought not to deny what is transparently true. They should defend their right to help influence American policy in a way they think is best for the country and themselves just as leaders of the National Association of Manufacturers would do. There is something ironic in anyone claiming to love his religious and cultural heritage and at the same time insisting that it has nothing to do with forming attitudes on social and political policy. More realistic was the view of Woodrow Wilson, who, when he was told what a pity it was that so great a man as Justice Brandeis should be a Jew, replied, "But he would not be Mr. Brandeis if he were not a Jew." Students of American life would be blind to ignore the influence of ethno-religious factors on politics in this country. It is almost as foolhardy to denounce it. To understand one phase of that influence is my aim in the chapters which follow.

CHAPTER II

Jeffersonians All

IN THE BEGINNING

EXCEPT in South Carolina, Jews in the colonies were not permitted to vote or hold office. Under the liberal Charter for Carolina written by philosopher John Locke in 1663, Jews voted in Charleston as early as 1702. Finally, in South Carolina suffrage requirements were enacted in 1721 which made it impossible for a Jew to vote or be elected to the Assembly. These restrictions were confirmed by the state legislature in 1759. Elsewhere in the colonies, even in liberal Rhode Island and Pennsylvania, the privileges of voting and holding office were limited to Christians, often merely Protestants, from the very beginning. Jews in New York did vote despite restrictive constitutional provisions until 1737, when in a disputed election, the Assembly ruled that Hebrews were not entitled to the franchise.

In effect, the political behavior of American Jews begins with the revolution. Relatively few Hebrews supported the British. In Newport, the established community dispersed rather than suffer the British occupation. Similarly, in New York most of the congregation of Shearith Israel left the city in order not to have to co-operate with Tory officials. Jews also supported the revolution far out of proportion to their numbers in Philadelphia and Charleston, two other cities with sizeable Jewish communities. Especially the Jews of Spanish and Portuguese extraction were wholeheartedly on the revolutionary side. Some were of the wholesale merchant class so adversely affected by British policies. But for many others economic interests would have dictated co-operation with the British, and hundreds made economic sacrifices to struggle against old-world rule. The reason is plain. Despite limitations on Jewish freedom in America, no Jewish community in Europe had yet achieved the degree of equality, freedom, and wealth possessed by the Jews in New York, Pennsylvania, South Carolina, and Rhode Island. The near future justified the faith which Francis Salvador, Aaron Lopez, Haym Solomon and others placed in the cause of American independence. American Jews were elected Congressmen and Governors and appointed to high administrative and judicial posts long before the first French, German, or English Jews were seated in their respective national legislatures.

Jewish political equality did not emerge immediately out of successful revolution. At the end of the war there were important discriminations against them in all of the states except Virginia and New York. In 1784, Jews first began to hear of a scholarly politician from Virginia named Madison. Opposing the fiery Patrick Henry, James Madison successfully defeated an attempt to make Christianity the state religion for Virginia. Two years later, Madison, Thomas Jefferson, and George Mason succeeded in removing all religious discriminations from the state constitution. It is difficult to call into the mind's eye the excitement with which Jews must have met Jefferson's Act to Disestablish the Anglican Church in Virginia, then the established Church in all colonies south of Maryland. Georgia followed Virginia in removing discriminations based on religion in 1789. Pennsylvania and South Carolina acted one year later. By 1790, one year after the first election of Washington, Jews had achieved political equality in the five states in which they were most numerous.[1]

---

1. Delaware removed religious tests in 1792, but Rhode Island, Massachusetts, Connecticut, North Carolina, New Jersey, and New Hampshire carried them into the nineteenth century. In North Carolina the constitution stipulated that persons denying Christ were ineligible for public office, until a new constitution was adopted in 1868. Disabilities against Jews were continued in New Hampshire until 1876.

General Washington was held in esteem by American Jewry as he was by nearly all of his countrymen. The separate messages to him from Jewish congregations in Newport, Philadelphia, New York, Charleston, and Richmond after his election showed the love and gratitude which Hebrews shared for the tall Virginian. The President, responding to the congratulations of Jewish congregations was warm and almost effusive, remarking that "the affection of such a people is a treasure beyond the reach of calculation."

While Jews might shower praises on Washington, they were not generally active in politics. Few could vote because of property qualifications even where they were allowed the suffrage. Still, relations between Jews and Gentiles were cordial and easy compared to the stresses of Europe, and the occasional Jew in public life was received without wonder. In Richmond there were not over seven Jews eligible for public office in 1785. Yet, Isaiah Isaacs received thirty-eight votes for a seat in Common Hall (the town council) and in 1788 increased his vote to fifty-nine, enough to be elected one of sixteen representatives.

JEWS TAKE SIDES

It took the French revolution to bring the American Jewish community actively into politics. No group was more fired by the controversy between the Jeffersonians—sometimes called Democrats, sometimes Republicans—and the Federalists over the French national struggle and the Napoleonic regime which followed. Under the revolutionary regime all discriminatory laws were abolished in 1791. Later, under Napoleon, Jews were emancipated wherever the armies of the French Republic were triumphant. At home the French were viciously attacked by Federalists and supported by the followers of Jefferson. Sensing their separateness from the Christian majority, Jews were especially outraged by the Alien and Sedition Acts of 1789, which were aimed at France and foreigners. When President Adams proclaimed a National Fast Day on May 9, 1789, most clergymen used the occasion to denounce the French Republicans. Not so with

Rabbi Gershon Mendes of Shearith Israel in New York who defended the principles of republicanism and democracy to his congregation.

It was not only the stormy argument over the events in France which prompted the Jews to side with Jefferson. A confluence of circumstances carried the Jewish community into the Jeffersonian camp almost as one man. There is no record of a single prominent Jewish opponent of the lanky, red-headed philosopher-politician. Jewish support for the republican cause was virtually monolithic. After all, it was Jefferson himself who had written the Disestablishment Act in Virginia. And it was his lieutenant Madison, soon to become the fourth President of the United States, who introduced the first amendment to the United States Constitution prohibiting the establishment of a national religion. Madison had even unsuccessfully introduced an amendment to the federal constitution to prohibit individual states from interfering with freedom of conscience. Had not Jefferson written to a Savannah rabbi that diversity in religion was the best thing for the country?

When the followers of Jefferson organized political clubs to support their hero, Jews could often be found working in their midst. Especially in New York, where the Jewish population had been stabilized for seventy years at about 400, Jews played a prominent role in politics. One of the founders of the Tammany Society in 1794, the Jewish merchant, Solomon Simson, became its President three years later. Naphtali Judah, another Tammany founder, was a President of Congregation Shearith Israel. Isaac Gomez, Isaac Levy, and Isaac Seixas were others who signed the original Tammany constitution. Mordecai Meyers and Noah Jackson, who later became a Grand Sachem, gave leadership to the young political organization.

Political activity in Charleston, the largest Jewish city of the time, was not as important as in New York, but Jews there were staunch Jeffersonians as everywhere. In Maryland, where Jews numbered fewer than 200 and were not allowed to vote or hold state office, the Etting brothers, Solomon and Reuben, worked for Jefferson's success. Reuben was rewarded in 1801 with an appointment as United States Marshal for Maryland. Some Hebrews even called their children after Jefferson and Madison, disregarding the Jewish injunction to name the newborn after deceased relatives.

The widespread entrance of Jews into American politics on one side raised ugly anti-Semitic attacks. When a slur against the Democratic Society of Philadelphia appeared in the Federalist paper, the *Gazette of the United States and Daily Advertiser,* one of the Jewish leaders of the Society, the French-born Benjamin Noanes, answered in a friendly paper that he was proud to be a Republican and a Jew. Writing that he was happy not to have forsaken the cause for which he fought as a Major in the war, he continued, "I am a Jew, and if for no other reason than that I am a Republican."

Noanes hit upon the primary reason for Jewish support of the growing Democratic clubs. Had there been no French Revolution, Jews still would have joined the Democratic faction in opposition to the policies of Alexander Hamilton and the Federalists. Hamilton's party was the party of the high-born, the privileged faction. Some Federalist leaders were strongly anti-Negro, anti-labor, and even anti-Semitic. Jewish experience in Europe with aristocratic or monarchical rule after which Federalists hankered had always been discouraging. Republican and democratic principles meant the liberty and respect which were indispensable to the growth of Jewish community life.

Of course, the anti-Semitism of some Federalists reinforced Jewish Jeffersonian proclivities. Because Solomon Simson, Assessor in the Second Ward in New York, was also Vice-President of Tammany, Federalist James Rivington wrote that members of the Democratic Club resembled their Shylock-like Vice-President. Rivington, a former Tory publisher and editor, sneered at Jewish influence in Tammany, but New York Jews were defended by their fellow Jeffersonians. Thomas Greenleaf, one of the first publicists

to work for Jefferson, printed anonymous replies to Rivington in Greenleaf's *Daily Advertiser* for December 17, 1795,
and two days later reprinted them on the front page of his
New York Journal. During the Presidential campaign of
1800 a Republican paper in Pennsylvania, the *Tree of
Liberty,* was labeled "the Jew press" by opponents of Jefferson. Again, Gentile supporters of Jefferson resented the attacks and said so. Whenever Jews were disparaged they found
Republicans at their side. One of their foremost supporters
was young Thomas Kennedy in Maryland, an ardent apostle
of Jefferson and Monroe, who fought for more than twenty
years to give Hebrews the privilege of voting and holding
office in his state. His opposition came primarily from Federalists in the state legislature, who even voted down a
memorial to permit the incorporation of a Baltimore Hebrew
Congregation.

The Federalist Party was doomed by its opposition to the
War of 1812, and offered its swan song at the famous Hartford Convention held between December 15, 1814 and Janu-
ary 6, 1815. In its last gasp the Party passed resolutions
proposing a constitutional amendment which would make
naturalized citizens ineligible to serve in Congress and
chastised the Republican Party for admitting such citizens to
places of honor and trust. What greater reason could American Jews have for continuing to give undiluted loyalty to the
party of Jefferson?

Nativism did not die with the Federalist Party. In Maryland the so-called "Jew Bill" to enfranchise the Jews was
made an issue in the campaign of 1819. At least one legislator
in Calvert County is supposed to have been defeated in his
bid for re-election because of his support for the measure.
Kennedy was warned to let the issue go. With fewer than
200 Jews in Maryland there were not enough votes in it. But
he relentlessly pressed his case until victory was won in 1826.
It was no surprise when Reuben Etting, grown wealthy as
founder of the Baltimore and Ohio Railroad, joined Kennedy in championing Andrew Jackson. So did Jacob I.

Cohen and Solomon Etting, the two other most prominent Jews in Baltimore, both elected to the city council immediately following the passage of the "Jew Bill."

Jackson and the new Democratic Party were the beneficiaries of Jewish devotion to Jefferson and Madison. In Richmond, Benjamin Wolfe and Joseph Darmstadt served as Democratic members of the town council. Solomon Jacobs, probably the most prominent Jew in the city, in addition to being President of Congregation Beth Shalome became Acting Mayor in 1818. Gustavus Meyers, born the year of Jefferson's first election, was recruited into the Democratic Party and lived to become a wealthy lawyer and the only Jewish member of the City Council between 1827 and 1855. In nearby Petersburg, Virginia, Samuel Mordecai, influential in the budding Jewish community, supported the hero of New Orleans. In Charleston a half dozen Jews served the Democrats in public office during the second quarter of the nineteenth century. And in Cincinnati, the Queen City of the West, where merely a half dozen Jews dwelt on the frontier, Joseph Jonas, one of the first Jewish pioneers, became one of the leading advocates of Jackson in Ohio.

It was in New York that Jews most energetically swelled the ranks of the Democrats. New York City was fast overtaking Charleston as the leading Jewish city in America, a position it was never to relinquish. Jewish influence in Democratic politics there grew with the years and the rapidly increasing Hebrew population. Two names stand out above the others. Emanuel B. Hart, a power in Tammany Hall for more than fifty years, received his training as a member of New York's volunteer fire department. His enthusiastic campaigning for Jackson in 1832 brought him a petty job in the Fifth Ward, where he became leader in less than five years. Hart later went on to bigger posts—to head Tammany's Central Committee, be elected to Congress, and serve in the national government in various capacities until he died at the age of eighty-eight in 1897. Foremost among the Jews of his day was Mordecai M. Noah, playwright, mystic, Zionist, and politician. Madison appointed Noah consul-general in Tunis in 1813 as a reward for political services. But Noah, who had a difficult personality, did not get along with Secretary of State Monroe, and soon returned to New York where he more actively pursued a political career. He edited and published a series of pro-Democratic newspapers, worked hard for Jackson, who appointed him Surveyor of the Port of New York, and became friends with Martin Van Buren for whose nomination and election Noah fervently conspired.

By 1840 a substantial majority of American Jewry—then about 15,000—helped form the coalition which "The Little Magician," Van Buren, so skillfully balanced to maintain power. When the charge of ritual murder was brought against the Jews of Damascus by the local Franciscan order at the instigation of the French consul, Van Buren acted swiftly to succor the Jews involved. As soon as the American consul at Alexandria communicated news of the attacks being made on the Jews in Damascus, Van Buren sent letters of instructions to the American consul there and the chargé d'affaires in Constantinople to use their good offices to protect the Jews, many of whom had been imprisoned, tortured, and murdered. It is hardly any wonder that the Jews of Richmond wrote to the President to express their heartfelt thanks. Van Buren's action was one of a series of events which fortified Jewish Democratic tendencies, and which made the Jews one of the most solidly Democratic groups in the country from the election of Jefferson in 1800 through the election of darkhorse James K. Polk forty-four years later.

CHAPTER III

The First Transition

DISILLUSIONMENT

THE LOYALTY of the Jews to Van Buren and the Democratic Party was not given as freely and completely to any Democratic Presidential candidate for nearly one hundred years. To be sure, the vast majority of Southern Jews remained true Democrats throughout the Civil War and during the ante-bellum period, but in the North a swift series of developments dissipated Jewish affection for the party of Jackson.

Perhaps as many as 100,000 German Jews emigrated to the United States between 1848 and the beginning of the Civil War. Many of the men had fought in the abortive revolution of 1848 and brought with them principles of political liberalism for which they suffered in the old country. These immigrants found much which dissatisfied them with the national leadership of both major parties. While the Democrats compromised with slavery in domestic affairs, the Whigs, in many states, were allied with the nativist movement. In foreign affairs, both parties had forsaken the Van Buren policy of aiding distressed Jews abroad. An anti-Semitic commercial treaty with Switzerland was negotiated during Fillmore's Whig administration and consummated on November 8, 1855 under Democratic President Pierce. American Jewry hardly noticed the treaty at first. The initial response to a protest in the weekly *Occidental and American Jewish Advocate* was negligible. By the fall of 1857 outbursts of complaint cropped up in various Jewish communities throughout the nation. Memorials were sent to Democratic President Buchanan and to leading Senators, to no avail. A committee in Baltimore issued a call for a national protest convention. Representatives came from as far west as Chicago and St. Louis. Finally, a delegation was sent to see Buchanan personally. Yet the President refused to renegotiate the treaty which permitted Swiss cantons to expel American Jews in accordance with their law.

Still a greater and more tragic rebuff came from Washington. In the Italian city of Bologna, Papal guards kidnapped a Jewish boy alleged by Papal authorities to have been secretly baptized four years earlier by a Catholic maidservant of the Mortaras (the child's parents). Mass meetings were immediately held in a number of cities protesting the Mortara affair. In New York City, where the Jewish population was probably not larger than 40,000, some 2,000 Jews attended a meeting which demanded that Buchanan intervene with the Pope. The President, through Secretary of State Cass, replied that the United States could do nothing. When reminded of Van Buren's action during the Damascus incident, Cass insisted that the Damascus case set no precedent.

The apathy in official Washington concerning the plight of the Mortara boy was a bitter pill for American Jewry. Jewish fear of Catholic power sharply accelerated. Already many immigrant Jews had joined the Whigs, because, as one observer put it, they probably "opposed a Catholic 'church militant' " even more than they feared nativism.[1] When the official New York Catholic paper, the *Tablet,* condoned the Mortara kidnapping, it hurt the Democrats with many Jews and Protestants. As one correspondent in the *Jewish Messenger* angrily commented, the difference between Van Buren's decision to intervene and Buchanan's withdrawal was that Mohammedans had no political power in the United States while Catholics were quite powerful.

---

1. Robert Ernst, *Immigrant Life in New York City, 1825-1863* (New York: King's Crown Press, 1949) , p. 167.

The Mortara episode made peculiar allies of some members of the anti-Catholic Know-Nothing Party and American Jewry. While certain individual Know-Nothing leaders were notorious Jew haters, such as Tennessee's "fighting parson" William Gannaway Brownlow and Massachusett's Senator Henry Wilson, anti-Catholicism was official party policy to which all members, more or less, were committed. An occasional Jew even supported the nativist position. The best known of these was Lewis C. Levin, who was born in Charleston in 1808. After spending his boyhood in Mississippi, Levin practiced law in Kentucky, Louisiana, and Pennsylvania where he finally settled. In Philadelphia he espoused the ideal of alcoholic temperance and had a hand in forming the Native American Party under which banner he was elected to Congress three times between 1845 and 1851. Levin, whose wife and children, strange to say, were Catholic, had no influence with his coreligionists, and the more typical Jewish attitude toward nativism was expressed by Dr. Isaac M. Wise, a leading reform Rabbi from Cincinnati, who lectured and wrote against the Know-Nothings. Jewish repugnance to nativism was as natural in the 1850's as it had been in Washington's time and has been ever since. M. C. Mordecai, a candidate for the State Senate from Charleston in 1855, typified the Jewish position when he cast off Know-Nothing support in a public letter, declaring that Jews themselves would not be safe if bigotry against Catholics should prevail.

These were the political choices which confronted German-Jewish immigrants as they came to this country during the early and mid-fifties. Some, repulsed by the Democratic association with slavery, chose the Whigs. In Chicago as many as half of the 200 Jews living in that Western settlement at mid-century were Whigs. Others, shocked by the marked affinity of the Whig Party for nativism, were unhappy with both parties and ripe for a third party movement. Still a third group followed the majority of their coreligionists and supported the Democrats.

DEMOCRATIC LOYALTIES

Tradition is a powerful force in politics. In New York City the Jewish community had been friendly with the Democratic leadership for four decades. During the 1840's and 1850's Democratic political leaders attended the important Jewish social affairs such as the annual dinner of the Hebrew Benevolent Society. Dinners in the late fifties for the Jew's Hospital, as it was called, were celebrated by the Mayor and his entourage of Democratic aldermen. Such friendships are not easily thrust aside. Many Jews in the North remained loyal to the Democratic Party right up until the Mortara affair and the election of 1860.

Probably the most prominent Jewish Democrats in the North were Emanuel Hart, who would not forsake his Tammany associations to vote for Fremont, and Rabbi Wise in Cincinnati, who, as an active anti-abolitionist, supported Buchanan in 1856. Through his weekly publication, the *Israelite,* Rabbi Wise urged compromise and deplored a radical solution to the slavery question. In Philadelphia, America's second-largest Jewish city, the Phillips brothers, Jonas and Henry, whose father had been a revolutionary war hero, supported Cass in 1852 and Buchanan four years later. Jonas, a member of the Board of Trustees of Congregation Michveh Israel, was the Democratic candidate for Mayor in 1847, and later refused Buchanan's offer of a district judgeship. Henry ran successfully as a Democratic candidate for the House of Representatives in 1856, where he urged the entrance of Kansas into the Union as a slave state. Edward Morwitz, a medical doctor, also advocated the election of Buchanan. Born in Prussia in 1815, Morwitz became an active Democrat soon after his arrival in Philadelphia, publishing the leading German newspaper in that city, *Die Demokrat.* Simon Wolfe Arnold was also recruited into the Democratic Party, remaining loyal after the war and serving as a Democratic elector for Seymour in 1868. Polish-born Stephen S. Remak was another Philadelphian to support Buchanan, a personal friend, who appointed Remak

U. S. consul at Trieste. The most energetic Jewish Democrat in the West was Edward Kanter. Kanter, born in Breslau in 1824, became a Van Buren Democrat when he came to this country and remained one throughout the troubled fifties, serving a term in the Michigan state legislature in 1857, running two times unsuccessfully for the office of State Treasurer, and acting as Secretary to the Democratic State Central Committee in 1860.

A NEW POLITICAL PARTY

By 1860, Democrats were the exception among Jews in the North. The German-Jewish refugees from the stillborn European uprisings of 1830 and 1848 especially welcomed the new Republican Party, the party of free men and free soil. The very name of the new organization was attractive to these German immigrants. Most of the Rabbis of the North opposed slavery, a few speaking out in their pulpits. Some became out-and-out abolitionists.

In the border city of Baltimore, Rabbi David Einhorn was a militant abolitionist. Einhorn and a member of his congregation, Leopold Blumberg, were forced to leave the city to flee from a secessionist mob. Moritz Pinner lived in equal danger in the border state of Kansas, where he edited a German-language abolitionist paper. In Philadelphia, Rabbi Sabato Morais met no extreme hostility, but some of his anti-Republican trustees did attempt to quiet his political views. But the new party was too popular, and his congregation supported his right to speak out.

Everywhere Jews were enlisting in the new Republican Party. In Chicago, four of the five organizers of a German mass meeting to start a local Republican organization were Jews. Philadelphia-born Moses Aaron Dropsie, formerly a Whig, was an ardent abolitionist who helped to organize the Republican Party in Pennsylvania. Dropsie's influence with his coreligionists was extensive. One of them, Solomon May, became the founder and President of the Sixth Ward Republican Club in Philadelphia. In still another Sixth Ward, the old Sixth of Rochester, newly arrived Jews joined the movement to save the Union and abolish slavery. Best known among these was Abram Stern, who worked tirelessly for Fremont in 1856 and who served for many years on the city's Common Council. In New York City, J. Solis Ritterband was elected President of the Young Men's Republican club. Two of his older friends, Abram J. Dittenhoefer and Sigismund Kaufman, played leading roles in the organization of the Party in Gotham.

The story of Dittenhoefer, who was a Presidential elector from New York in 1860 and for twelve years the Chairman of the Republican Central Committee in New York, is especially dramatic. Born in South Carolina, the young college graduate left the Democratic Party at the age of nineteen, deciding that as a Jew he could not countenance slavery. His father, a prominent merchant zealous for the political success of his son, urged Dittenhoefer to remain a Democrat. But the boy's conversion was too deep to trifle with. He recalled how his Democratic leanings were irrevocably changed when he read of the debate in the Senate between Republican Ben Wade and Judah P. Benjamin, the Jewish pro-slavery Senator from Louisiana. When Wade called Benjamin an "Israelite with Egyptian principles," Dittenhoefer felt compelled to help the Republican Party.

Kaufman, who was also a Republican elector for Lincoln in 1860, mixed legal ability with strong idealism. Born in Darmstadt, he had taken part in the 1848 revolution, and after coming to this country became active in civic and Jewish affairs. He wrote for the *Staats Zeitung* and was President of the German Society in New York. As an abolitionist he was naturally drawn to Lincoln, and campaigned unstintingly in both elections. Later the President offered Kaufman the post of Minister to Italy, but the New Yorker preferred to stay close to politics at home, where he was an important figure in the distribution of federal patronage.

Several Jews in the West were leaders of the Republican Party at its inception. From Missouri to the Republican

Convention in 1860 came Moritz Pinner, and from Louisville, Kentucky, Lewis N. Dembritz, who was one of three to place Lincoln's name in nomination. Lincoln's old friend from Quincy, Illinois, Abraham Jonas, took the stump for Fremont, and then for the "prairie lawyer" himself. Like Lincoln, and unlike most Jews, Jonas had been a Whig, and served as such in the Kentucky legislature in 1828, 1830, and 1833. In nearby Chicago a former Democrat, Henry Greenbaum, an alderman in 1855, switched to the new-born Republican Party and later became a personal friend of Lincoln. According to Greenbaum, most of the prominent Jews in Illinois supported the great emancipator. In far off Oregon, Maier Hirsh, who came to the United States from Wurttenberg in 1852, became a merchant in Salem and helped push the Republican Party on its way. Hirsh remained to become a power in western Republican politics, serving as a delegate from Oregon to the Republican national convention in 1864.

IN THE SOUTH

Southern Jewry for the most part steadfastly served the ideals of the South. Among the Jews in Charleston, many of whom were prosperous and owned slaves, there is no record of a single abolitionist. Prior to the break with the North, Southern Jewry appears to have been divided on the nullification issue. In the famous South Carolina nullification convention in 1832, the four Jewish delegates evenly split their votes. Later, Jews were similarly divided over the question of secession. But even those who first opposed secession stood with the South when the break came. Philip Phillips, formerly a member of the Alabama State Legislature and a representative in Congress from Mobile, opposed secession while in Washington but returned home immediately following the outbreak of hostilities. Douglas Democrat Edwin Moise opposed secession but remained loyal to the South, serving as Speaker in the Louisiana House of

Representatives at the beginning of the war. Fire-eating Southerners such as Raphael J. Moses did their best to promote a strong pro-slavery states rights point of view. Moses, who had been a delegate from Florida to the Democratic convention which nominated Lewis Cass for President in 1847, helped lead his adopted state of Georgia into war and later enlisted with his three sons in the Confederate Army. Gustavus Meyers, by this time one of the best known and most respected Jews in the South, was loyal to Jefferson Davis, and subsequently became one of the sureties on the $100,000 bail bond put up for the Confederate President.

Two of the staunchest supporters of the South had been leading political figures in Louisiana before the war. Henry Hyans was Lieutenant Governor from 1856 to 1860. The more prominent politician was Judah P. Benjamin, who, after achieving some fame as a lawyer, was elected to the Senate in 1852. Since Benjamin was indifferent to his religion, and was, in fact, buried in a Catholic cemetery, his influence on coreligionists was slight. His influence in national politics, however, was large. Whig President Taylor offered him the cabinet post of Attorney General, and President Pierce nominated him to a seat on the Supreme Court. However, Benjamin, whose peddler parents sold dried fruits in one of the little streets near Cheapside, London, won widest fame as a loyal member of the Confederate cabinet of Jefferson Davis.

The Jewish community in New Orleans, unlike the one in Charleston, was not completely unified in its support of the South. Many Union sympathizers went North. But some spoke out openly in New Orleans itself. Rabbi Bernard Illowy of the German Congregation became friendly with General Banks, the Commander of the Federal Army of Occupation, and delivered a favorable sermon on Lincoln, as did Colonel P. J. Joachimsen in the Polish Synagogue. New Orleans gave the South Judah P. Benjamin, but it rewarded the North with Michael Hahn. Hahn, born in Bavaria in 1830, became a Democrat in Louisiana, supporting Stephen Douglas for the Presidential nomination in 1860. But he always opposed slavery and secession. After the war began he took an oath of allegiance to the United States, and in December 1862 was elected to Congress to fill an unexpired term. While he never joined the radicals in Washington, he firmly supported Lincoln. Later, on February 22, 1864, Michael Hahn was elected the first Republican Governor of the state of Louisiana on the Free Soil ticket, and remained an active Republican for the rest of his life.

The Hahns and Illowys were the obvious exceptions in the South, even among Jews. Wherever Southern influence was strong most Jews acquiesced in the Southern point of view. Southern tradition even carried into the growing Jewish community of San Francisco. Many Californians, such as San Francisco's Abraham C. Labatt and Solomon Hydenfeldt, were transplanted Southerners. Both of these men were born in Charleston, as were so many of the prominent Jews of the day. Labatt emigrated directly to California as a young man and was elected alderman in San Francisco in 1851. Hydenfeldt served in the Alabama State Legislature before going West. There he proposed an amendment to the State Constitution to prohibit the further immigration of slaves into Alabama, and upon failing moved to San Francisco the following year, the spring of 1850. Hydenfeldt believed slavery was wrong, but he was a strong states rights man and his sympathies were with the South in its tribulations. Opposition from "Northern" Californians prevented his election to the United States Senate in 1851, but he was nominated and elected as a Democrat to the Supreme Court of California later that same year. Hydenfeldt, who was active in Jewish affairs, presided over the small Mortara protest meeting in San Francisco. Despite Buchanan's inaction and his own opposition to slavery, he remained a Democrat, actively supporting Breckenridge in 1860.

The candidate of the South was the most popular candidate in San Francisco in 1860, receiving even more votes than Douglas and almost twice as many as Lincoln. With some four thousand souls in the city altogether, there cannot have been more than forty Jewish adults, but most of them appear to have had at least lukewarm sympathies for the South, and an unusual number were active in local politics. Like Hydenfeldt, M. J. Newmark was a delegate to the Democratic state convention which supported Breckenridge. Abel Stearns was elected to the State Assembly that same year. But the Jewish tendency in California to sympathize with the Southern cause was based on affection for friends and relatives caught up in a struggle for regional survival, not on agreement with slavery. When Lincoln was assassinated the Hebrew Congregation in San Francisco met for prayers, as did Jewish congregations everywhere.

CHAPTER IV

The Republican Years

FATHER ABRAHAM

THE POSITIVE Jewish response to Lincoln almost transcended political and regional boundaries. Jewish leaders from the North and South who had once opposed the odd-looking frontier lawyer grudgingly recognized his statesmanship. Even Rabbi Wise, who remained a friend of the copperhead leader Clement L. Vallandigham, paid tribute to Lincoln's greatness before the President was murdered.

Jews had their special reasons for coming to love Lincoln. It was not just that the President had a number of Jewish friends. So did most other important politicians. Nor was it Lincoln's eloquence or statesmanship, although these too had their appeal. What drew Hebrews to Lincoln more than anything else was the President's vast humanitarianism. Lincoln's charity was so profound that he could not carry the slightest shred of anti-Semitism, and, indeed, showed that he understood the special sensitivity of Jews to discrimination. When Congress passed a law providing that Chaplains be Christians, Lincoln promptly responded to the entreaties of Hebrew citizens and intervened to have the law changed. Then came the infamous anti-Semitic Order No. 11 issued by General Grant giving all Jews in the Department of Tennessee twenty-four hours to leave the area. In trying to rid the border states of tradesmen who were dealing with the enemy, Grant singled out Jews, not all of whom were peddlers by any means. The President first learned of the expulsion order from Cesar Kaskel, a small shopkeeper from

Paducah, Kentucky who made a hurried visit to Washington. On hearing of the order, Lincoln immediately wrote a message to Commander-in-Chief Halleck directing its cancellation. Such actions were bound to touch Hebrews favorably in the South as well as the North, and Lincoln appears to have been widely respected by most Jews everywhere.

One fact stands out beyond the positive Jewish response to Lincoln. A disproportionate number of Jews in both the North and the South supported the Union in war and the Republican Party at the war's end. The trend was decidedly against the Democrats. The change in the reputations of August Belmont and Joseph Seligman illustrate the declining fortunes of the Democrats as well as anything else. When the Civil War began, August Belmont, the financial agent of the Rothschilds in America, was the best-known German Jew in this country. Although he supported the Union in war, he remained an active Democrat, and even served as Chairman of the National Democratic Committee. After the war Seligman became the most prominent Jew in the United States. He and his brother Jessie were personal friends of Lincoln and Grant, who later offered Joseph the Secretaryship of the Treasury Department. Joseph Seligman was an imposing figure at several important Republican mass meetings during the war, including the famous Cooper Union meeting.

At the war's end there were about 200,000 Jews in the nation, and the vast majority of Jewish voters supported the emergent Republican Party. Abraham Kohn, who had helped to form the party organization in Chicago, became city clerk there. Lewis Solomon was elected Republican State Senator from the same city in 1870. Sigismund Kaufman continued to be a power in New York politics, receiving the nomination for Lieutenant Governor in 1870. The success of this social democrat was partly due to the wooing by the Republican Party of German and Jewish votes. In Philadelphia Leonard Meyers helped to build the Republican Party and was sent to Congress for seven sessions. The newer

Jewish communities, such as the one in post-Civil war Rochester, tended to be strongly Republican. Only in far off Utah, where the Republican Party was the Mormon Party, did the Jews join in efforts to start an opposition organization. Samuel Kahn of Salt Lake, a leading wholesale grocer and staunch supporter of Lincoln throughout the war, was one of the prime movers behind the new Liberal Party in 1870. Five other Jews, including Simon Bamberger, elected nearly fifty years later as the first non-Mormon Governor of Utah, were among the founders and active members of the Liberal Party. But the situation in Salt Lake was peculiar. Under ordinary conditions most Jews sided with the Party which ended slavery and won the war. Even in the South during the ante-bellum period a small number of Jews became active Republicans. However, most of the dwindling Southern Jewish population joined their fellow Southerners in opposing reconstruction governments and supporting such unreconstructed rebels as Wade Hampton of South Carolina in his quest for the Governorship.

REPUBLICAN TENDENCIES

One obstacle which Republican politicians had to overcome was the alleged anti-Semitism of General Ulysses S. Grant. During the weeks which followed the issuing of Order No. 11, mass meetings were held in New York, Philadelphia, and Chicago demanding the General's dismissal. Feelings were bound to subside somewhat by the 1868 election campaign, but the order was made a campaign issue nonetheless. Many letters were addressed to newspapers reminding readers of Grant's action, and an attack against him appeared in a twelve-page pamphlet entitled *General Grant and The Jews*. But Grant himself gave assurances that he regretted the order, and the controversy could not turn the Jews from their Republican course. During his administration the rough and simple soldier went out of his way to be friendly to Hebrews. In addition to offering his friend Joseph Seligman a cabinet post, he appointed General Edward S. Solomon Governor of the Territory of Washington, offered the post of Governor of the District of Columbia to Adolphus S. Solomons, who turned it down because he could not work on the Sabbath, and appointed Benjamin Peixotto, head of B'nai B'rith, as consul-general to Rumania in the hope that Peixotto might succeed in mitigating the growing persecution of Jews in the Balkan country. Whether or not these appointments were calculated to solidify the increasing Jewish Republican vote, they tended to have that effect.

A large number of Jews continued their Democratic affiliations, but outside of the South not many new voters became Democrats. Emanuel Hart, a power in Tammany Hall for nearly half a century, never changed his allegiance even though he served Republican Presidents as Commissioner of Immigration in New York in the 1870's. Nor did Solomon Hydenfeldt, who remained active in Democratic State conventions in California through 1871. These were Democrats of a lifetime, Jews with memories of Van Buren and Jackson. Few were left of that stamp. The swelling Jewish population was composed mainly of new German and Polish immigrants and of the children of those who came in the 1840's and 1850's.

Between 1860 and 1890 the American Jewish population increased from somewhere between 200,000 and 300,000 to approximately 900,000. Perhaps slightly more than half of the newcomers came from East Europe. During this period Jews divided their loyalties between both parties, but the predominant affiliation remained Republican. Two factors probably sustained Jewish Republican tendencies more than any others. First, the idealism and tradition of Lincoln still punctuated the orations of Republican politicians. After all, the Democratic Party in the North was discredited as the Party of slavery. Second, Republican Presidents and their Secretaries of State showed a readiness to act to relieve the misery of persecuted Jews in Eastern Europe. Grant's appointment of Peixotto was followed by the reminder which

Hayes's first minister, William Evarts, gave to Rumania in 1879 that the United States feels a responsibility for Hebrews in foreign countries. When the news of Russian pogroms reached this country in 1882, Frederick T. Frelinghuysen, Republican President Arthur's Secretary of State, urged the Russian imperial government to stop the persecution. Later James G. Blaine, perhaps the leading Republican of the time and then Secretary of State under Benjamin Harrison, instructed the American minister to Russia to exert his influence against measures threatening the Jews. To be sure, these actions had bipartisan support, and similar efforts were exerted during the Democratic Administration of Grover Cleveland; but with the exception of eight years, Republicans controlled the executive power during this period and credit for humanitarianism was generally cast on to the party in power. Of course, the motivation for such action was not only humanitarian. It was often political. When John Hay, McKinley's Secretary of State, protested to Bucharest in 1902 against Rumanian oppression, he was consciously courting the Jewish vote. His protest was widely read in the synagogues that year and may have helped the Republicans in the congressional elections. It made no difference that Hay cynically and privately wrote, "The Hebrews—poor dears! All over the country they think we are bully boys."

Everywhere Jews were finding their way into politics. Some received diplomatic and administrative posts. Some were elected to high office. Others became leaders in party organizations. They served widely in both parties, but most of them appear to have been Republicans. From far off Oregon, where the Hirsch brothers were active in Republican politics, to New York City, where the Seligmans, Dittenhoefer, and Kaufman held sway, Hebrews were still attracted to the party of Lincoln. Maier Hirsch continued to be active in Salem politics. His brother, Solomon, was Benjamin Harrison's Minister to Turkey. A third brother, Edward, served as a State Treasurer and State Senator in the far western state.

Jews could be found at every level of Republican Party organization. Immediately after the Civil War Benjamin Raphael became the Republican leader in Greenpoint in Brooklyn. A half mile away Ernest Nathan, and then after him Jacob Brenner, were the Republican leaders in Williamsburgh. Abraham Oppenheimer succeeded Raphael as leader in Greenpoint although the Jewish vote there was still negligible and the population was predominantly Irish and German. Nathan was eventually elected Chairman of the Republican Executive Committee in Kings County (The city of Brooklyn), and when he retired in 1889, Israel F. Fisher succeeded him.

The most powerful organization man by far was "Boss" Abe Ruef of San Francisco. The Jews have had few political bosses of city-wide stature. Besides Ruef, there have been Bernstein and Maschke of Cleveland, both Republicans, and more recently Jacob Arvey of Chicago, a Democrat. Ruef, in his own city, was the most powerful of them all. Born in San Francisco of French parents, possessed of a keen intellect, he made an excellent record at the University of California. Paradoxically, Ruef started in politics as a Republican reformer, and was one of the founders of the Municipal Reform League. Personal ambition soon crushed his earlier idealism. Organizing a new political party, the Union Labor Party, Ruef rose from precinct captain to czar almost overnight. Reaching the height of his power at the Republican state convention in 1906, he toppled swiftly because of personal involvement in a series of public scandals. While Ruef was not a pious Jew, and was disparaged by coreligionists outside of San Francisco, most of the Jews of the city supported him during his troubles. His political career and lifelong ambition to go to Washington as a United States Senator were finally smashed by his conviction for bribery and extortion in 1908.

Other Republicans did go to the capital to sit in the national legislature. Michael Hahn was returned to the House of Representatives from Louisiana in 1885. Four years later Nathan Frank of St. Louis was elected to Congress on the Republican and Union Labor tickets. Frank, who was the founder and owner of the *St. Louis Star,* was an active delegate to the Republican national convention in 1896 and ran unsuccessfully three times for the United States Senate. The wealthy glove manufacturer, Lucius Littauer, was elected to the House of Representatives from Gloversville, New York, for five consecutive terms from 1897 through 1912, and was a delegate to all Republican state conventions for fifteen years beginning in 1897 as well as to four national conventions. From Brooklyn came Israel Fisher in 1894. He was preceded by Edward Einstein of New York City in 1879, who thirteen years later was an unsuccessful candidate for Mayor. The self-appointed major domo of Washington Jewry was lawyer Simon Wolfe, a dedicated Republican and friend of Republican Presidents from Grant to Roosevelt. Wolfe, whose devotion to Jewish causes made him President of the expanding B'nai B'rith organization, and whose fidelity to the Republican Party won him the consul-generalship in Egypt under Garfield and Hayes, invariably took it upon himself to speak for American Jewry at the White House.

SOME WERE DEMOCRATS

Despite its success among Hebrews, the Republican Party had no monopoly on Jewish political loyalties. Republican Jews in Congress might look across the aisle and find about as many of their brethren there as on their own side. Bavarian-born Leopold Morse was active in Boston Democratic politics, from which city he was elected to Congress in 1877, '79, '81, and '83. Alfred Meyer represented Louisiana in the House of Representatives from 1891 through 1908 until he died. New York City sent Isidor Straus to the House in 1894 to fill a vacancy, and Jefferson M. Levy was elected to a regular term in 1899. Levy was a nephew of Commodore Uriah P. Levy, a legendary figure in American Jewish history and good friend of Thomas Jefferson.

Some Jews, such as Henry M. Goldfogle, were recruited into Tammany politics near the end of the century and made rapid political progress. Goldfogle was a delegate to the Democratic national conventions in 1892 and 1896, and was elected to Congress in 1910 where he served for sixteen years. Baltimore-born Isador Raynor was the most powerful Jewish Democrat in Washington. He was elected to the Maryland General Assembly in 1878, to Congress ten years later, and was finally chosen as United States Senator in 1905. Later, Raynor turned down two opportunities to receive the Democratic nomination for Vice-President.

With Raynor in the Maryland legislature was Martin Emerich, who had been active in Democratic politics for more than a decade, and who was eventually sent to Congress from a Chicago district in 1903. His friend, Chicago's Samuel Alschuler, was an unsuccessful Democratic candidate for Mayor in the midwestern metropolis only three years before. Other Jewish Democrats ran for state and city offices. Edgar M. Johnson, a descendant of the second Jewish family to settle in Cincinnati, was a popular political figure in Ohio and was nominated for Lieutenant Governor in 1881. Jews participated freely in Cincinnati politics. In 1900 the two opposing candidates for Mayor were Jews, Republican Julius Fleishman and Democrat Alfred M. Cohen. Fleishman was elected Mayor for two successive terms. Cohen later became the first Democrat in forty years to win election to the State Senate from Hamilton County more than once, and was rewarded with the nomination for Governor in 1911.

Although Philadelphia was safe in the vise of Republican "Boss" Senator Matthew Quay, an unusual number of Jews were active Democrats. The Democratic legacy of the Phillips brothers, Morwitz, Arnold and Remak was carried forward by Henry S. Frank, Simon Muhr, and Emanuel Furth. Furth served in the state legislature for several years and figured in the debates of 1894 to abolish the Pennsylvania "blue laws."

Heavily Democratic New York City was fast becoming the most Jewish metropolis in the world. Although many Jews were Democrats, only a few of them, such as Goldfogle, were attracted to the Tammany organization, then reeling from the blows of successive scandals. Some were drawn to the organization through friendship, such as the wealthy real estate operator Andrew Freeman, who, as a favor to his close friend Richard Croker served for a while as Treasurer of Tammany in 1897. But most prominent Jewish Democrats, such as Henry Morgenthau and the Straus brothers, preferred to call themselves Cleveland Democrats, and remained independent in local affairs. Morganthau enlisted with the Democrats as a law student when his young friend Michael Sigerson ran for the State Assembly in 1876 on the same ticket with Presidential Candidate Tilden, who had become Morgenthau's hero as Governor of New York. Morgenthau remained a national Democrat all his life, while opposing Tammany in his own city. Oscar, Isador, and Nathan Straus were raised as boys in Talbottan, Georgia, where they naturally acquired Democratic sympathies which they brought with them to New York City. In New York they made a fortune as great merchants, eventually founding Macy's department store. While all three brothers gave active support to Cleveland in both of his campaigns, they would not work with Tammany. In fact, Isador, who was elected to Congress in 1893, soon broke with the Democrats on the issue of free silver, and both Isador and Nathan refused to accept Democratic nominations for the Mayor of the city. Isador, before his death on the Titanic, became the President of the Educational Alliance set up to facilitate citizenship for immigrant Jews and to keep them away from the Tammany tiger. The most famous of the brothers was the youngest, Oscar Straus. When President Cleveland, at the suggestion of Henry Ward Beecher and others, appointed him Minister to Turkey in 1887, Straus began a career of high public service which made him the best-known and most widely respected Jew of his time.

Obviously not all Jews were Republicans in the four decades which followed the Civil War. At the turn of the century Jews were still widely divided, the slight major party preference remaining with the Grand Old Party. While most of the English-Jewish periodicals tended to be Republican, the growing Yiddish press was sharply divided in its political loyalties. In New York City, the *Tagblatt* and the *Morning Journal* were Republican, but the *Warheit* and the *Day* supported the Democrats, while the important *Daily Forward* was Socialist.

Exclusive preoccupation with Jewish political behavior ought not to obscure the fact that politics for countless numbers of Hebrews was remote and unimportant. The Jews never displayed the zeal and ability for political organization that still marks the Irish-Americans. Hebrews channeled their energy into other kinds of activities—the arts, commerce, entertainment, and trade union organization.

THE NEW VOTERS

Between the election of William McKinley and the beginning of the first World War nearly two million Jewish immigrants came to the United States. Most of them were refugees from the anti-Semitism and poverty of Eastern Europe. They crowded the tenements in the slums of New York and to a lesser extent Boston, Chicago, and Philadelphia. Since 1890 approximately two-thirds of America's Jewish population has centered in these four metropolitan areas. A majority of the immigrants became peddlers and laborers or worked as cutters and tailors in the needle trades. To a large number of them the parties of the radical left—particularly socialists—provided the only political answers. The rest confined themselves to a choice between major parties. Of these, more probably chose Republican than Democratic candidates in every Presidential election from 1900 to 1928 with the exception of 1916.

Republicans were preferred primarily for three reasons. First, Jewish immigrants listened to the older and wiser Jewish heads already here, most of whom were Republicans; second, they felt enormous gratitude toward the Republic which granted them refuge, gratitude which was turned toward the administrations then in power; and third, they did not like the Irish, the group which for more than half a century had formed the core of the Democratic Party in the East.

THE FIRST ROOSEVELT

As the immigrants arrived from peasant villages in Russia and Poland, many of them attributed their good fortune to Republican Presidents then in power. The change from ignorance to public education and from pogroms to electoral privileges was often ascribed to McKinley, Roosevelt, and Taft. One sixty-one-year-old Jewish housewife in Boston's Jewish section recalled that she and her husband always voted Republican until 1932. "After all," she said, "Theodore Roosevelt's name was on the immigration paper which let us in."

It is difficult to picture the incredulity of newly arrived Jews, many thousands of them illiterate, and still many more penniless, when they heard that President McKinley appeared on September 16, 1897 with his cabinet for the laying of a cornerstone for a Washington synagogue. They must have been glad in their hearts at the actions of philo-Semitic Theodore Roosevelt and William Howard Taft. Roosevelt was especially revered by American Jewry. The President could be rough and even cruel. His own autobiography often shows him unable to sympathize with weak individuals or groups. But his friendship for Jews was large. As far back as 1895 when he was Police Commissioner in New York he brought smiles to Jewry. When the notorious German anti-Semite, Pastor Hermann Ahlwardt, arrived in New York to address a large public meeting, the Police Commissioner with tongue in cheek assigned only Jewish policemen to protect him.

As President, Teddy Roosevelt performed many kindnesses to Jews. He was the first President in history to invite the Rabbinical Conference of the United States to visit him in the White House. Twice he predicted that a Jew would be elected President of the United States. In 1902 he appointed Oscar Straus to succeed ex-President Harrison as American representative to the Arbitration Court at Hague. Four years later he brought Straus into his cabinet as Secretary of Commerce and Labor, stating "I want to show Russia what we think of the Jews in this country." Soon after, at a banquet held in Straus' honor, Mr. Roosevelt forgot his intentions toward the Imperial Government of Russia. In his speech the President boasted that he named Straus because of his ability and devotion to high ideals. "I did not name him because he was a Jew. . . . I would despise myself if I considered the race or religion of a man named for high political office. I would have named Mr. Straus if he had been a Methodist or of French blood. Merit and merit alone dictated his appointment." The toastmaster at the dinner was the wealthy financier, Jacob Shiff, Roosevelt's good friend and frequent correspondent. But Shiff was deaf, and did not hear a word that T.R. said. When Shiff's turn to speak came, he embarrassed the blustery President by recalling how Roosevelt had called him to Washington specifically to tell him that he wished to appoint a Jew to his cabinet and to ask Shiff to recommend an able man who would be acceptable to American Jews. Roosevelt swallowed his embarrassment and American Jews generally rewarded him with friendship and votes.

During their administrations Roosevelt and Taft tried many times to ameliorate the persecutions of Jews in Europe. When prominent Jews drew up a petition to send to the Czar protesting the massacre of coreligionists in Kishinev in 1903, the Rough Rider accepted the document and sent

it off forthwith. It made no difference to their feelings for
T.R. that His Imperial Majesty would not deign to see it.

Refugees kept coming to the United States by the tens
of thousands. By the 1904 election there were about 700,000
Jews in New York City alone. Probably not more than one-
tenth of these were even eligible to vote. Still, the Jews
formed a sizeable voting group which politicians felt it
prudent not to ignore. Jews themselves were sensitive to the
wooing of political leaders, and especially in the Anglo-
Jewish press editorials deplored the tendency to write or
speak of a "Jewish vote." Anglo-Jewish weeklies such as the
widely read *American Hebrew* endeavored to stay out of
politics, but in 1904 its publisher, Philip Cowen, felt obliged
to promote Roosevelt's candidacy. Cowen tried to dodge
the classic question of whether or not Jews should vote as
Jews by agreeing that while there must be no such thing as
a Jewish vote, Jews ought not refrain from voting for a man
who "has indisputably done things that entitle him to the
good-will of our people." No big national issues divide the
candidates anyhow, argued the *American Hebrew,* so why
not vote for the man who has proved his friendship for Jews.
The most prominent Jews of the country, Oscar Straus,
Judge Mayer Sulzberger, and Jacob H. Shiff, all supported
Roosevelt. Shiff wrote that he could not believe that any
eligible Jew would fail to vote for the President. Of course,
some eligible Jewish voters not only failed to vote for him,
but actively worked for Alton B. Parker, the Democratic
candidate, or for Socialist Eugene V. Debs. In Boston's Ward
8, Martin Lomosney was able to keep most of his Jewish
voters in the Democratic line. However, a majority of Jews
elsewhere agreed with Cowen's advice and voted to re-elect
the President.

One of the big issues for Jews during the next few years
was the eighty-year-old anti-Semitic commercial treaty with
Russia under which the Imperial Government refused to
honor the passports of American Jews. A vigorous outcry of
Jewish protest followed the announcement by Secretary of

State Root in 1907 that the State Department would not issue passports to Americans unless the Russian government consented to their admission. Root was forced to revise his position, and both party platforms in 1908 promised "the just and equal protection of all our citizens abroad." Meanwhile, Jews were fleeing from the persecution of Eastern Europe in unprecedented numbers. In 1906 and 1907 alone, more than 300,000 Jewish refugees arrived from Europe.

The genial William Howard Taft, former Secretary of War and the heir apparent to Roosevelt, was the Republican nominee in 1908. His opponents were Socialist Eugene Debs, and the Democrat from Nebraska, William Jennings Bryan, then a candidate for the third time. The passport issue came up again and again. Taft spoke in Jewish Brownsville in Brooklyn, reiterating his desire to make all American passports good in Russia. Bryan wrote a letter to the *American Hebrew* saying that American Jews ought to have the same protection as American citizens anywhere abroad. Secretary of State Root sent a letter to Republican Jacob Shiff saying he would insist that Russia not discriminate against American Jews who wished to travel there. Shiff, Straus, and Sulzberger backed Taft just as they had T.R. in 1904.

As yet, not many Jews were prominent in politics. Among those who tried for political careers, slightly more appear to have entered through the Republican than the Democratic door. For every rising Democrat it was possible to name two or three Republicans. While Tammany sent Goldfogle to Congress and Isidore Raynor was at the height of his Congressional career tossing oratorical barbs at Roosevelt for alleged usurpation of legislative power, Republicans Israel Bacharach of New Jersey and Julius Kahn of California exercised considerable power in the House of Representatives. In New York, Republican Isaac Siegal was only a few years away from a Congressional career, and in the 18th Congressional District in the Bronx, J. F. Spingarn waged a lively Republican campaign for the lower house.

As immigrant Jews were enfranchised, Jewish political behavior became increasingly important to political leaders. Vital judicial and administrative posts had to be given to Jews just as they were given to every other sizeable minority group. Oscar Straus continued as Secretary of Commerce and Labor until 1909. President Taft tried to persuade the brilliant Nathan Cardoza of New York to accept a federal judgeship. For many immigrants gratitude toward Taft for his friendship continued to be mixed up with thankfulness for simply being in America. In a Charles Angoff novel of Jewish life in Boston in the early 1900's, one aging grandmother, Bobbe, actually credits the wonders of American plumbing to President Taft. When she first learned that there was no charge for hot and cold running water she remarked, "President Taft must really love the poor people. . . . May he live to 120 years." Writes Angoff, "Chaskell once tried to tell her that President Taft had nothing to do with it, that inside water facilities were a part of the American city home for many years before Taft became President, but Alte Bobbe dismissed his talk with, 'That may well be, but a President, if he didn't like the poor, could put a stop to these water pipes, and President Taft doesn't.' "[1]

THE FEELING WAS MUTUAL

Another factor in favor of Taft and the Republican Party was the close association of the Democratic Party in the North with Irish Catholicism. When the immigrant Jew arrived in New York, Chicago, or Boston he usually found that Irish bosses controlled the local machinery of government. In New York it was Tammany's Charlie Murphy and his Irish lieutenants. In Boston the spoils of power were divided among Martin Lomosney in the West End, Pea Jacket Kennedy (to be followed by James Curley) in the

1. Charles Angoff, *In The Morning Light* (Boston: The Beechurst Press, 1952), p. 293.

South End, John P. Fitzgerald in the North, and P. J. Kennedy in the East End.

The Irish were in and the Jews were out. And although Martin Lomosney, ever sensitive to population trends, tried to cultivate the Jewish vote by nominating and electing Jewish candidates to the State House of Representatives from Jewish districts, his successors were zealous in keeping Jews out of important posts in the Democratic organization. As the years went by the Irish Democratic leadership in Boston made less and less effort to win the unneeded votes of the fractious and troublesome Jews. Wherever the Jews of Boston moved they found the Democratic organization tightly controlled by Irishmen. When they moved to Dorchester-Mattapan and Ward 14 in the twenties, the only committee and convention posts they could seek were in the Republican organization. While at least twelve delegates elected to the Republican state convention in 1926 from Ward 14 were Jewish, only one delegate to the Democratic state convention was a Jew. Despite the shift of Jewish voters to the Democratic Party in 1932, all Democratic State Committeemen from districts embracing Ward 14 were Irishmen, while all of their Republican rivals were Jews.

In New York, Charles Murphy successfully enlisted the support of Jewish politicians, and Tammany had its Jewish following, but the returns reported for Jewish districts show that most Jews resisted the blandishments of coreligionists in the service of Murphy. Murphy's successors, like those of Lomosney, did not court the Jews. Although the Jews rapidly outnumbered the Irish in the Democratic districts of Manhattan, few positions of leadership in the organization were parceled out to them. As late as 1923 there were only five or six district leaders out of thirty-six who were Jewish.

But there was more to Irish-Jewish friction than merely the fact that the Irish were in and the Jews were out. Differences in habit, custom, and temperament as well as in ritual and religion contributed to the mutual hostility of Erin and Israel. After watching Irish politicians in Boston's

West End attempt to win the votes of newly arrived Russian Jews, one settlement worker wrote, "The social relations of the Irish and the Jew are not very cordial. There seems to be a special antipathy ordinarily on the part of the Irish for the Jews."[2] One eighty-year-old resident described in 1952 in heavy accent how the efforts of Lomosney's workers to bribe him with tobacco and whiskey into voting the Democratic ticket prompted him to become a Republican instead. A great New York settlement worker put it, "the intellectual Jewish East Side for the most part did not comprehend the game played by political leaders. . . ."[3] All this redounded to the benefit of Republican candidates during the first three decades of the century.

After Taft was elected in 1908 he failed to take steps to abrogate the discriminatory Russian trade treaty as he had indicated during the campaign. Jewish leaders were naturally disheartened. Finally, he invited representatives of the most important Jewish organizations to confer with him in February 1911, when to their disappointment he explained that abrogation of the treaty would be unwise from the point of view of American national interest. Protests continued and were climaxed by a public meeting in Carnegie Hall in New York City. The audience was addressed by the Democratic Speaker of the House of Representatives, Champ Clark, and by the rising Governor of New Jersey, Woodrow Wilson.

WOODROW WILSON

Woodrow Wilson became the first Democratic Presidential candidate to crash the Republican hold over the Jews in half a century. His idealism and professorial background both commended him to Jewish voters. The *Jewish Advocate* in Boston, where the Jewish population had grown

2. Robert A. Woods, ed., *The City Wilderness: A Settlement Study by Residents and Associates of the South End House* (Boston: Houghton Mifflin & Co., 1899), pp. 134-135.

3. Mary Kingsbury Simkovitch, *Neighborhood—My Story of Greenwich House* (New York: W. W. Norton & Co., 1938), p. 65.

in thirty-five years from 5,000 to well over 75,000, declared
for Wilson in the 1912 election, stressing that "Jews should
support a man like him, who has made culture the shining
purpose of his life." Life-long Republican Jacob Shiff joined
Wilson in the campaign. Louis Marshall, the President of
the new American Jewish Committee, supported Taft, but
Henry Morgenthau was induced back into politics by Wilson's compelling idealism. Morgenthau had remained aloof
from politics ever since the Tilden campaign in 1876, amass-
ing a fortune through business and financial enterprise. In
1911 he was attracted to the progressive Governor across the
Hudson River, and in an effort to find out more about him
invited him to speak at the Free Synagogue in New York.
After the speech Morgenthau asked Wilson if he were really
a candidate for the Presidency, to which Wilson replied that
he knew a good deal more about the United States than he
knew about New Jersey. This was enough for the financier.
He gave his time and money to both Wilson campaigns,
becoming Chairman of the Democratic Finance Committee
in 1912.

There was one other major candidate for the Presidency
in 1912—Theodore Roosevelt. Remaining loyal to T.R. was
Oscar Straus, running himself for Governor of New York
on the Progressive ticket. But the Rough Rider had lost
some of his luster by 1912, even among the Jews. Conservatives were alienated by his Columbus, Ohio speech attacking
the judiciary. Liberals saw an opportunity to vote for a gen-
uinely progressive Democratic candidate other than William
Jennings Bryan. Socialists preferred the perennial Presidential aspirant, Eugene V. Debs, who ran well in Jewish
districts everywhere. All candidates opposed literacy tests for
immigrants, the one issue which interested the Jews as Jews,
since such tests would have excluded an estimated twenty-five
per cent of the Jewish immigration at the time. When the
election came Jews split their vote four ways.

There was obviously no such thing as a Jewish vote in
the sense that all Jews voted for this or that candidate. Yet,

Jews were constantly preoccupied with denying to themselves and others that such a vote existed. The number of Jewish voters in New York was carefully estimated at over 110,000 in 1910, 68,000 in Manhattan alone.[4] Jews then represented about 13 per cent of the eligible voters in the city. Many politicians courted Jews for political purposes. William Sulzer represented a Jewish East Side district in Congress for seventeen years and made a special point of playing up to his Hebrew constituents. Some Jews, particularly the American-born Jews of German stock, resented the special appeals which politicians such as Sulzer constantly made. They also deplored the way in which administrative and diplomatic posts were parceled out to ethnic and religious groups. Oscar Straus was not alone in lamenting the growth of hyphenated political organizations. Yet, he had been criticized himself for having accepted a third appointment as Minister to Turkey from Roosevelt, a post he had held under Cleveland and McKinley. When Wilson offered the Embassy at Constantinople to Morgenthau, the latter conveyed some of the resentment which coreligionists felt at having this particular post put aside for Jews—as if Jews could not aspire to other jobs, only this one. Morgenthau told the President that all the Jews he consulted urged him to decline the appointment.

It was the German Jews who were especially anxious not to form Jewish political clubs or develop anything like a Jewish political point of view. Back in August 1891 the German-Jewish *Jewish Chronicle* of Boston ridiculed the efforts of President Benjamin Harrison to woo Jewish voters by publicly acknowledging the receipt of a present of *matzos* from a Jewish Rabbi in San Francisco. Russian Jews in Boston organized a variety of political clubs. The Young Men's Hebrew Political Club tried to foster good citizenship and naturalization. The Democratic Jews of the North End and

---

4. Abram Lipsky, "The Number of Jewish Voters In New York," *American Hebrew*, Vol. XCII, No. 1 (November 1, 1912), p. 5.

the Third District Independent Club actually took stands on candidates and issues. Russian Jews did not frown on the use of Jewish names in politics or mass meetings, as did their German brethren.

One rising Tammany politician from the East Side challenged the German point of view in an answer to the *American Hebrew*. Jonah J. Goldstein, destined to run for Mayor of New York thirty years later as a Republican, wrote that Jews ought to be in politics frankly as Jews in order to receive the political recognition the group deserves. Most Jews tended to agree with Straus and Morgenthau in theory and Goldstein in practice. How could the growing immigrant population fail to be pleased when Sulzer carried by a unanimous vote a resolution he introduced in the House of Representatives denouncing the Russian trade treaty! Similarly, most Jews were gratified when Morgenthau changed his mind and accepted the post at Constantinople where he used his influence to help Palestinian Jews. And the vast majority of them were thrilled when Wilson called financier Bernard Baruch to the White House for advice or when it was speculated that Louis D. Brandeis might receive a cabinet appointment.

If Jews had not rewarded their friends with votes they would certainly be different from any other group which ever crossed the American political scene. When Democrat James M. Curley ran for Mayor of Boston in 1913 he was aided by a strong Jewish vote, perhaps as much as 85 per cent, as a reward for his pro-immigration efforts in Congress. The same bounty was paid to David I. Walsh, Democratic candidate for Governor, whose opponent was Augustus P. Gardner, a leader of the anti-immigration forces in Congress. But Jewish enthusiasm for Wilson transcended parochial interest. From multimillionaire Bernard Baruch, of whom Secretary of the Navy Josephus Daniels said, "Loyalty to Wilson was Baruch's first name," to the skull-capped immigrant, the dignified and stern professor captured the loyalty of hundreds of thousands of Hebrews. After his re-election in 1916 the *American Hebrew* glowed with editorial praise for his administration. Thousands of Jews were pacifists and socialists and could not countenance Wilson any more than they could Hughes, but for the first time in at least sixteen years and perhaps for the first time since 1856 more Jews voted for a Democratic candidate for President than voted for the Republican nominee.

Wilson's victory was paralleled by the success of a growing number of Democrats elsewhere. In the Far West two Jews who received their start in politics with insurgent minor parties were elected Democratic Governors of their respective states. Both were prosperous merchants. Yet each allied himself with a small minority group which challenged the dominant Republican Party. Moses Alexander was born in Bavaria in 1855 and emigrated to Missouri as a young man, where he established a business in Chillicothe. There, he was elected Mayor on the Union Labor ticket. After moving to Boise, Idaho, his interest in politics led to his election as Mayor on a nonpartisan slate. Subsequently his fortunes were tied to the minority Democratic party. An unsuccessful candidate for Governor in 1908, he was elected six years later and re-elected in 1916 when he appeared on the same ticket with Wilson.

Simon Bamberger's political history is even more unusual. One of the founders of the Liberty Party in the now dead city of Corinne, Utah in 1869, Bamberger, who campaigned for Abraham Lincoln, lived to be elected the first non-Mormon and first Democratic Governor of Utah. Grown wealthy in mining and banking, the German-born Bamberger, who was President of his Congregation in Salt Lake, was noted for his pro-labor views.

Most Jewish officeholders were still Republican, but by 1916 the number of elected Jewish Democrats had grown substantially. The two Hebrew Congressmen elected from New York City were Republican Isaac Seigal and Socialist Meyer London. Two of the three Jews in the New York State Senate were Republicans, but there were nine Democrats in the Assembly to five Republicans and two Socialists. In Chicago, rapidly becoming the second largest Jewish city in the nation, Ulysses S. Schwartz, named after the Republican General, was a Democratic City Councilman. A young lawyer named Samuel Pincus and businessman Michael Rosenberg were beginning active careers in local Democratic politics. But the major Jewish political figures in Chicago were Republicans. Circuit Court Judge Julian W. Mack owed his appointment to President Taft, and Samuel A. Ettelson and Emanuel Eller were close aides of Republican boss Bill Thompson. Ettelson, then in the State Senate, later became corporation counsel for Chicago when Thompson was Mayor. In Congress itself the two most influential Jews were Republicans, old-guarder Israel Bacharach from New Jersey, and the senior Republican on the Military Affairs Committee, Julius Kahn of California.

THE APATHETIC TWENTIES

The Census for 1920 showed that over two million persons in this country gave Yiddish as their mother tongue, an increase of almost 23 per cent over 1910. Not all new citizens rushed to exercise their voting privileges. There was considerable apathy in local and even national elections. Returns show that participation was usually low in the most Jewish assembly districts in New York. The only contact most Russian immigrants had with government was at the local level, and it was often unpleasant. In Boston's South End, Jews were stopped by the police from performing weddings on Sunday in licensed halls. In New York, peddlers without a license were often rebuffed by the local constabulary. In some places school children even received bad grades for being absent on Jewish holidays. For the most part the immigrants did not depend on the organization for jobs and free medical advice, but on other more prosperous and established coreligionists.

The 1920 Presidential election was received with considerable indifference. Despite the impact of Wilson's New

Freedom and The League of Nations on Jewish voters, his
death and the temporary disappearance of the issues he
raised blocked any formidable switch in major party loyalties.
The Indiana State Democratic Committee tried to impute
anti-Semitism to the distinguished-looking Senator Harding
from Marion, Ohio, because he had voted against the confirmation of Brandeis' appointment to the Supreme Court;
but probably few Jews heard of the allegations and fewer
still were impressed. Nineteen-twenty was a Republican year,
and, except for the ever present Socialist minority, Jews were
no less Republican than the rest of the country. The number of Jews elected to Congress increased from six to eleven,
all Republicans except for Socialist Meyer London from
New York. The two Jewish Democrats up for re-election,
Henry Goldfogle in New York and Adolph Sabath from
Chicago's West Side, went down to defeat with Presidential
candidate James Cox. Eugene Debs, the Socialist candidate,
ran better than he ever had done before, polling nearly a
million votes and making substantial gains in Jewish
districts.

In this pre-Hitlerian age it must have seemed to most
Jews that there were no crucial issues dividing the major
parties. For the confirmed Socialist the choice was easy. For
others it was easier to stick with the Republican Party than
do anything else. The country was prosperous. Jews were
moving ahead. Republican politicians, supported by occasional addresses from Taft and Coolidge praising American
Hebrews, continued to recruit the Jewish vote which Irish
Democrats spurned. Taft's speech on "Anti-Semitism in the
United States" was printed and distributed widely among
Jewish leaders. Harding's administration was lackluster and
marred by corruption, but when the President died, the
B'nai B'rith News saluted him for being devoid of prejudice
and welcomed his successor, Calvin Coolidge, as "a sturdy
protector of law and order." The newer and less talkative
Chief Executive continued the personal friendship for Jews
which appears to have been traditional among Republican

Presidents. His address at the laying of a cornerstone for the Jewish Community Center in Washington, D. C., was called by the *Jewish Advocate*, "the most remarkable tribute to the Jewish people in America" ever expressed by any President.

Jewish apathy greeted the campaign of 1924. The platforms of the two major parties were almost identical. There was some bad feeling against Harding for having signed the first anti-Semitic and anti-Italian immigration act, but Coolidge could not easily be blamed for that since the act had bipartisan support as well as opposition. In 1924, Coolidge ran ahead of Wall Street lawyer John W. Davis in most Jewish wards and assembly districts. Only the Jewish Socialists sustained excitement during the campaign. The Progressive candidate, Robert LaFollette, received the Socialist endorsement and ran ahead of both Coolidge and Davis in the most Jewish districts in Manhattan (17th), the Bronx (4th), and Brooklyn (23rd).

THE SECOND TRANSITION

Stray straws in the wind indicated an impending Democratic renaissance among Jewish voters. In 1922 more Jewish Democrats than Republicans were elected to Congress for the first time since the Civil War. One of these was Meyer Jacobstein, Professor of Economics from the University of Rochester, who was to serve three terms in the House of Representatives, and later, as economic consultant with the Brookings Institution in Washington, be instrumental in formulating the idea of a National Recovery Administration Act to Franklin D. Roosevelt.

Despite the election of Coolidge in 1924, three new Jewish Democrats were sent to Congress from New York City: Samuel Dickstein, Sol Bloom, and Emanuel Celler. The election of Bloom and Celler from two Jewish congressional districts which had heretofore been Republican was another sign that Republican sway over the Jewish population was crumbling. Sol Bloom was elected to the House from the heavily Jewish 19th congressional district in uptown Man-

hattan. Until 1924 the district had returned Republican
Walter M. Chandler for seven consecutive terms. When
Congressman-elect Samuel Marx died two weeks after the
election, Charles Murphy, Democratic boss of New York
County, asked Bloom to run because in the late Congressman's words, "I was an amiable and solvent Jew." Though
Bloom beat his Republican opponent in a special election
by a mere 145 votes, his victory was a portent of things to
come. Across the East River a young Jewish lawyer, now the
senior Democrat on the House Judiciary Committee, was
persuaded to run for Congress from a predominantly Jewish
district in Brooklyn. Emanuel Celler's plurality of 3,111
votes was not large, but as such it was a sign of the times.
Democrats were making gains among Jews.

The self-consciousness which made American-born Jews
of German origin keep out of politics in the latter half of
the nineteenth century prompted Russian immigrant Jews
to seek recognition in politics. When Louise O. Aloe lost a
close election for Mayor of St. Louis, the *Jewish Daily Bulle-
tin* complained that anti-Semitism played a role in her defeat. In March, 1925, the *Denver Jewish News* complained
that Jews were being discriminated against in politics; and
two months later the Jewish *Day* in New York said that the
appointment of Jews to high office under Roosevelt and
Wilson was a higher compliment than the beautiful senti-
ments expressed by Coolidge in cornerstone-laying ceremonies. The *Brooklyn Jewish Chronicle* in November openly
suggested that a Jew be appointed as successor to Judge
Gavin of the Federal District Court. It was true that Jews
were underrepresented as such. Only eleven sat in the House
of Representatives. None sat in the Senate. Not one of the
great political bosses of the day was a Jew. But the reason
was not anti-Jewishness alone. Jews continued to choose
paths other than politics for careers in America. And more
than two-thirds of the four million Hebrews in the country
were products of new immigrations, still greenhorns.

Each election brought more Jews to high public office,

and most of the new figures were Democrats. In 1926, five Jewish Democrats were elected to Congress, three Republicans and one Socialist. The most politically powerful Jews were still Republicans. Maschke headed a strong organization in Cleveland. Isaach Bacharach, first elected to Congress in 1915, was probably the most powerful political leader in Atlantic City, New Jersey. Benjamin L. Rosenbloom of West Virginia retired from the House of Representatives to make an unsuccessful bid for the Republican Senatorial nomination. Florence P. Kahn was elected to Congress from San Francisco to replace her husband, Julius, who had served since 1899 with the exception of only two years, and who had been Chairman of the powerful House Committee on Military Affairs. In Cincinnati Murray Seasongood, a militant fighter for reform and the City Charter movement, found himself elected Mayor, the third Jewish Republican Mayor of that city since the turn of the century. In Wisconsin the smiling Jewish peddler, Sol Levitan, whose motto was "don't say nothing against nobody" was re-elected for a third consecutive term as State Treasurer. And in New York, Albert Ottinger survived the Democratic landslide which swept Alfred E. Smith into the Governor's chair, and was re-elected Attorney General. Nevertheless, Ottinger did not win the support of most Jewish voters. Almost overnight the appealing East Sider with the derby hat, Al Smith, was turning the Jews of New York into good Democrats.

For New York Jews the turning point came in 1924. Al Smith ran for Governor. He cut heavily into the usually high Jewish Socialist vote despite the popularity of candidate Norman Thomas. And Thomas ran ahead of Theodore Roosevelt Jr., the Republican candidate, in some of the most heavily Jewish assembly districts. Almost half of the Jews in the country, slightly more than a million, lived in New York City. Their enthusiasm for Al Smith was shared in other large Jewish cities during the 1928 campaign for the Presidency. In Chicago's Ward 24 where Davis had failed to win a plurality four years before, Al Smith received 74.5

per cent of the vote against victorious Hoover. In the Bronx 4th A.D., Brooklyn 23rd A.D., and Manhattan 17th A.D. where Davis had been the recipient of one out of every three Jewish votes cast, 69 per cent, 66 per cent and 71 per cent of the total vote was recorded for Smith. Over in the West Bronx, in the 2nd A.D., embracing more well-to-do neighborhoods than those across the Concourse, the Democratic vote went up from 36 per cent in 1924 to 67 per cent for Smith in 1928. Even in Boston's Ward 14, where the local Jewish political leadership remained exclusively Republican, Al Smith received 61 per cent of the vote.

The Smith vote in New York, Chicago, and Boston did not mean that Jewish Republican strength toppled all along the line and in all cities. Especially where the dominant organization was Republican, as in Cincinnati, Cleveland, Philadelphia, and Stamford, or where Jewish organizational involvement was Republican, as in Boston, Jewish enrollments and Republican strength in state and local elections remained high. In Ohio the head of the Hamilton County Executive Committee, Gilbert Bettman, was elected Attorney General. Louis Marshall, the head of the American Jewish Committee, was still prominently identified with Republican leaders, and Samuel Koenig was the Republican leader of Manhattan, a position he was to hold until 1932. From San Francisco Mrs. Kahn was sent back to Congress for a third term. Murray Seasongood was re-elected Mayor in Cincinnati and Harry Bacharach Mayor of Atlantic City.

The trend was against the G.O.P., however. The growing Jewish support for the Democratic party manifested itself in many ways. In 1930, six of the eight Jews elected to Congress were Democrats. Merely ten years before the entire Jewish delegation of eleven had, except for one Socialist, been Republican. National issues began to emerge between the two parties which had repercussions in state and local contests. Democratic leaders seemed a little bit more anxious to end prohibition, a little bit more wary of restrictive immigration laws, a little more willing to take drastic steps to relieve unemployment and aid labor than their Republican counterparts. These things appealed to American Jewry. Of three Jewish Governors elected in 1930, two were Democrats and the third, Julius L. Meier, an independent. Meier was born of Bavarian parents in Portland, Oregon, where he became a successful lawyer. His former law partner, George Joseph, died suddenly after having been nominated for Governor on the Republican ticket. Like Joseph, Meier was a progressive with advanced ideas on social and economic policy.

The other two Jewish Governors, Arthur Seligman and Henry Horner, were also the sons of German immigrants. Seligman, born in Sante Fe, New Mexico, became rich as a merchant and banker, and was elected Democratic Mayor of Sante Fe in 1910. From 1911 to 1920 he was Democratic State Committee Chairman, then national committeeman from New Mexico, and finally he was elected Governor in 1930 in what had been a Republican state. In Illinois, Henry Horner was carried into office by a large plurality. His Bavarian-born grandfather had been one of the earliest settlers in Chicago. Horner studied law, established a large and lucrative practice, joined the Democratic Party, served as a local judge, and in 1930 was elected to the highest office in the state.

In Horner's native Chicago the Jewish population combined with other recent immigrant groups to back the Democratic Party. A virtual revolution had taken place in Chicago politics in merely a decade. Just ten years before, Harding had carried Cook County by more than 450,000 votes and Big Bill Thompson's Republican organization seemed unbeatable. In 1931 Anton J. Cermak, a Bohemian, became the first foreign-born Mayor of Chicago. Cermak was a master at nationality politics. He enlisted the support of Jews and other groups who resented Thompson's sneering at "Tony and his pushcart." Thousands of Jews were or had been peddlers, too, and Cermak won their votes.

In New York a crippled Democratic Governor with a huge head and a broad Harvard "A" was re-elected Governor on the Democratic ticket, running handsomely in all Jewish districts, even a little better than Al Smith in 1926. Franklin Roosevelt was popular throughout the state, but not as popular as his Jewish running mate, Herbert Lehman, whose plurality was the largest on the ticket. There was no mistaking the tide. Jews were returning to the Democratic Party in a big way.

CHAPTER V

The Democratic Return

On a cool fall evening just forty years after President Taft assured an Anti-Defamation League audience that Jews "make the best Republicans," Adlai Stevenson, Democratic candidate for President in 1952, told a cheering Jewish crowd in Boston's Ward 14 that Jews make the best Democrats. As already written, the conversion of Jews from good Republicans to good Democrats did not occur overnight. It was more rapid in some cities than in others, but it was general and it was steady, and by 1932 the Jewish commitment to Roosevelt was great indeed. In Chicago there was a marked shift to F.D.R. in the Jewish sections of the windy city—Garfield Park, Albany Park and Lawndale. In the twenty most Jewish precincts of Ward 24 (over 90 per cent Jewish), Roosevelt received 84.7 per cent of the vote. In the same districts the Jewish Democratic candidate for re-election as Governor, Henry Horner, won 96 per cent of the vote, running almost 12 per cent ahead of Roosevelt. In Boston's Ward 14 the Democratic vote went up from 61 per cent in 1928 to 84 per cent in 1936. In the Jewish neighborhoods of New York the swing to Roosevelt was just as complete. In New York City, Gubernatorial candidate Lehman and Presidential nominee Roosevelt ran equally well. Both received a little over 92 per cent of the two party vote in the 17th Assembly District in Manhattan. Actually, the crusading Democratic Senatorial candidate, Robert F. Wagner, led the ticket in the 17th A.D., running ahead of both Roosevelt and Lehman. His electoral prowess was all the more remarkable because his Republican opponent was George Z. Medalie, a Buffalo Jew active in philanthropic affairs who had been United States Attorney for the Southern District in New York. In other Jewish districts Lehman usually led the ticket by a small margin, but in every one of them Wagner gave Medalie a sound thumping.

Every local Democratic candidate did not receive the same warm Jewish response which was given to Wagner, but the shift to the Democratic Party was radical. The long-range switch from Republican allegiance in the 1920's to the current predominantly Democratic loyalties of American Jews is dramatically expressed in the party enrollment figures for Ward 14 in the city of Boston, a consistently heavy Jewish area from 1924 until this day. In 1928, 78 per cent of the voters there were Republican. By 1952, only 14 per cent of the enrolled voters in Ward 14 called themselves Republican. Of course, the nation as a whole, particularly urban voters, experienced a similar shift during the same period. But there were exceptions, and the switches that did occur, except for Negroes, were hardly so pronounced. In 1952 the percentage of primary electors voting in the Republican primary in Boston's Italian Ward 3 was only 2.1 per cent less than it had been in 1926; in Irish Ward 15 it was 2.6 per cent less; in Yankee Ward 5 it was 2.4 per cent more; but in Ward 14, 75.2 per cent of the primary voters in 1926 were Republicans, in 1952 merely 10.1 per cent—a drop of 65.1 per cent!

Although the shift in Boston was more exaggerated than elsewhere, the same pattern prevailed in other cities. In 1942 Boss Ed Flynn of the Bronx, the most Jewish county in the United States, claimed that the Bronx was also the most Democratic county north of the Mason-Dixon line.[1] A year after the publication of Flynn's book, a top political reporter in New York asserted that Brooklyn was "the strongest Democratic unit in the nation."[2] The fact is that wherever Jews have lived in great concentration since 1936 they have

---

1. Ed Flynn, *You're The Boss* (New York: Viking Press, 1947), p. 220.
2. Warren Moscow, *The Empire State* (New York: Alfred Knopf, 1948), p. 11.

been heavily Democratic. In Paterson, New Jersey's Fourth Ward, then about 70 per cent Jewish, Landon received barely 30 per cent of the Presidential vote. In the most Jewish precincts in the nation, twenty-four precincts in Chicago bounded by West Roosevelt Street, South Pulaski, South Homan, and West 16th St., Roosevelt won 97.1 per cent of the votes cast for President. In New York County's 17th A.D., F.D.R. garnered better than 90 per cent of the ballots. Four years later in 1944, 95 per cent of the Jews in Boston's Ward 14 picked Roosevelt. During the last fifteen years there has been no group in the country more Democratic than the Jews. The marked Democratic attachment in national elections has turned close congressional districts into sure Democratic areas. Whereas Sol Bloom won his first election by a plurality of 145 votes in 1922, he consistently won by more than 50,000 votes during the forties. Between 1922 and 1952 Emanuel Celler increased his plurality from 3,111 votes to 90,000.

The Jewish return to the Democrats was not limited to New York, Chicago, and Boston. The results of national surveys conducted by the American Institute of Public Opinion and by the National Opinion Research Center at the University of Denver show that more than ninety out of every one hundred Jews in the nation voted for Roosevelt in 1940 and 1944.[3]

THE JEWS AND ALL THOSE OTHERS

The Jewish shift to Roosevelt in 1932 and 1936, while it was unusually large, did parallel the results in the nation

3. The Denver results are analyzed by S. J. Korchin, *Psychological Variables in the Behavior of Voting*, Ph.D. Thesis (Cambridge: Harvard University, 1946). The Gallup results are presented and analyzed by Wesley and Beverly Allinsmith, "Religious Affiliation and Politico-Economic Attitudes," *Public Opinion Quarterly* (Fall 1948); by Liston Pope, "Religion and Class Structure," *The Annals of the American Academy of Political and Social Sciences* (March 1948); and in an unpublished monograph by Robert T. Bower, "Voting Behavior of American Ethnic Groups 1936-1944," (New York: Bureau of Applied Social Research, Columbia University, September 1944).

as a whole. A core element in the great Roosevelt coalition which Roosevelt had forged to win sweeping victories in 1932 and 1936 were the children of the last great American immigration. The Jews were no different in this respect than the Italians or the Poles who also warmed to the prospect of a New Deal.

But the Presidential voting behavior of the Jews was peculiar in three major respects: First, the Jews as a group persisted in their Democratic attachment long after large numbers of other minority groups became disenchanted. While the peak Roosevelt strength for other groups was reached in 1936, it was not reached until 1940 and 1944 for America's Jewish population. Moreover, the entire pattern of the return to the Democrats was different for the Jews than for others. Second, the Jews as a group made much greater economic progress than the other minority groups in the Roosevelt coalition. By 1944, the results of national surveys revealed the Jews were among the best paid and best educated of all denominational groups. On occupational prestige scales the Jews were consistently rated higher than the most successful Republican denominational groups—the Congregationalists, Presbyterians, and Episcopalians.[4] Third, the results from surveys also showed that the Jews constituted the only ethno-religious group in which differences in Democratic-Republican strength could not be correlated with differences in occupational prestige, amount of income, or education.[5]

DEMOCRATS WITH MONEY

Taking the second peculiarity first, it appears that American Jews swung to the party of Jackson just at the very time they began rapidly to climb the class ladder. As Democrats, the Jews were alone among the well-to-do ethno-religious

4. Allinsmith, *op. cit.,* p. 385. Pope, *op. cit.,* pp. 84-91. Pope reports that "Distribution (by classes) of the Jewish group is very much like that of the Episcopalians; a majority of the members of both still come from the middle and upper classes. . . ." (p. 86) .
5. Bower, *op. cit.,* p. 16. Korchin, *op. cit.,* p. 93 and pp. 194 ff.

groups. According to one study, American Jews actually comprised the highest status group of any of the seventeen denominations under consideration.[6] Jews were the only denomination whose votes could not be predicted from knowing the income or occupational or educational status of the group. *Table 1* shown below reveals the extent to which this was true in 1944.

TABLE 1

COMPARISON OF HIGH STATUS RELIGIOUS DENOMINATIONS
PER CENT DEMOCRATIC IN 1944

(Adopted from Wesley and Beverly Allinsmith)

Denomination	% FDR	Educational Rank	Occupational Rank	Economic Rank
Jews	92.1	3	1	4
Congregationalists	31.4	1	2	1
Episcopalians	44.6	2	4	3
Presbyterians	39.9	4	3	2

One other similar study showed the Jews first in occupational status, fourth in educational and income status, and voting 92.8 per cent Democratic in 1944.[7] The Jews were very different from other minority groups in the Roosevelt coalition in that they were economically successful.

WHETHER THEY ARE RICH OR POOR

The Jews were very different in another way. Analysis made of the 1940 and 1944 elections by Robert Bower and Sheldon J. Korchin showed that differences in Democratic strength within all religious groups except the Jews could

6. Allinsmith, *loc. cit.*
7. Pope, *loc. cit.*

be attributed to differences in economic status.[8] The poorer Jews, the laborers, the uneducated were no more Democratic than their richer, college-educated coreligionists in business or the professions. A later study of the results of a survey of college graduates done for *Time* magazine showed that even within the high status occupations, such as the professional and executive positions, Jews were found to be in higher income brackets than Catholics and Protestants.[9] Yet, so far had the Jewish swing to Roosevelt transcended class lines that a mere six per cent of these college graduates called themselves Republican.[10]

THE PATTERN OF ATTRACTION AND WITHDRAWAL

The Jewish return to the Democrats not only was more complete than the swing of any other ethno-religious group, but it started later and, with the exception of the Negroes, has persisted longer than for the others. The pattern of attraction and withdrawal for different ethnic groups in the city of Boston shows that other minority groups in Boston were most Democratic in 1928 and 1932, while Jews did not achieve full Democratic strength until 1940 and 1944. Roose-

---

8. Bower, *op. cit.*, pp. 16, 17. Korchin, *loc. cit.* Both Bower and Korchin separated ethno-religious groups into class categories. In order to get large enough samples of each ethnic group, Bower was obliged to combine nine separate cross-sectional surveys. He found that the Jews were the only group studied which did not respond in more or less the same way to four social factors—age, education, income, and sex. For 1940 and 1944, income made little difference to Jewish voters while education made none at all.

Korchin studied the results of a stratified national sample of 2,564 Americans of voting age who were interviewed before the 1944 election, 2,030 of whom were re-interviewed after the contest was over. Korchin did not describe the vote behavior within each of the major religious or ethnic groups at different class levels. However, he did separate respondents into five "religio-economic" groups. Since he found that the poor Jews and Catholics combined gave Roosevelt only 82.1 per cent of their vote while Jews from all five classes cast 86.5 per cent of their votes for F.D.R., it is reasonable to conclude that Jewish enthusiasm for Roosevelt transcended class lines.

9. Ernest Haveman and Patricia Salter West, *They Went to College* (New York: Harcourt Brace & Co., 1952), pp. 187-188.

10. *Ibid.*, p. 194.

velt's percentage vote increased each time he ran in Jewish Ward 14, while it fell off in Irish Ward 15 in 1936 and 1940 and dropped in Italian Ward 3 in '36, '40, and '44. In New York the pattern was similar. The high water mark of Democratic power in non-Jewish sections such as Richmond came in 1928, 1932, and 1936. In the Bronx Second A.D. and nearly all Jewish areas the Democratic zenith was reached in 1944.

The pattern of attraction to and support for Democratic Presidential candidates also shows that the Jews usually moved in the opposite direction from other elements of the Smith-Roosevelt coalition. While the Jewish high point in Democratic strength was reached in 1944, Roosevelt won less than 65 per cent of the vote in Ward 15 (Irish) and Ward 3 (Italian) in Boston. In Richmond county, less than one per cent Jewish and about 50 per cent Italian, the vote for the Democratic candidate dropped below 50 per cent for the first time since 1924. In 1948 the non-Jewish minority of the Roosevelt coalition increased their Democratic vote while the Jewish vote fell off. In 1952 the Jews and Gentiles reversed directions. In the Jewish areas Stevenson maintained the Truman vote while widespread defections from the Democrats occurred in Irish, Italian, and Polish sections.

The great moment for Irish and Italian Catholic Democrats actually came in 1928 when Al Smith, a son of Irish-Catholic immigrants, was the Democratic standard bearer. Irish wards in Boston have never been as Democratic since. The most politically articulate group in American society finally had an opportunity to vote for one of its own for the highest office in the land. If anything, Irish enthusiasm for Smith decelerated the Jewish return to Democracy. It was Roosevelt, not the Liberty Leaguer Smith, who was most congenial to Jewish aspirations, as Jews showed by their resounding Democratic vote in 1936.

Just as 1928 marked the arrival of America's immigrant and minority Catholic population, so 1944 was a year of triumph for America's Jews. The end of the war was in sight.

Hitler was all but smashed. The archenemy of world Jewry and all of his allies, foreign and domestic, had been discredited. There were diplomatic assurances that Germany's surrender would be unconditional and that war criminals would be punished. Friendship with the Soviet Union, with the regime which was alleged to have ended pogroms and anti-Semitism, was popular and applauded. The widespread Jewish opinion on the need to destroy Hitler and befriend the Soviet Union had apparently been accepted by everyone. The flood of anti-Semitism which had swept the nation like a mighty ocean tide in the late 1930's was, it seemed, permanently dammed. And in every city in the United States where Jews were concentrated they expressed their gratitude and satisfaction by casting a prodigious vote for Franklin Roosevelt.

Jews marched to the polls almost as one in 1944 to express their thankfulness to the architect of the victory over Nazism. Whatever the type of city or neighborhood, wherever Jews were concentrated, marginal voters and habitual nonvoters voting for the first time joined the regulars in casting ballots for F.D.R. In every Jewish precinct and ward more Jews voted than ever before, just as the Catholics had turned out in 1928. In middle-class neighborhoods, in upper-class neighborhoods, in big cities, in the suburbs the Jewish vote for Roosevelt was overwhelming. As may be seen in *Table 2,* the extent of the Democratic vote in Jewish areas in Chicago did not vary with the economic character of the neighborhoods as much as it did with the extent of their Jewishness. In heavily Jewish precinct 31, Ward 49, which is in well-to-do Rogers Park, Roosevelt received 89.6 per cent of the ballots cast. Just around the corner in non-Jewish precinct 47 he won merely 39.4 per cent. In the three most Jewish precincts of Ward 48, a fine section called Uptown, where nearly half of the male population is employed in professional, technical, or managerial capacities, F.D.R. won 82 per cent of the vote. In the Ward as a whole 55.3 per cent of the vote went Democratic.

TABLE 2
THE DEMOCRATIC VOTE IN JEWISH DISTRICTS IN CHICAGO IN 1944

District	% F.D.R.	Characteristics of population and area*
Ward 24 (22 most Jewish precincts)	95.9	Estimated 91% Jewish; median income $2,923; median rental $45.39; occupational structure lower-middle and lower class.
Ward 40 (5 most Jewish precincts)	90.6	Estimated 91% Jewish; median income $4,191; median rental $48.29; occupational structure upper-middle class.
Ward 49 (precinct 31)	89.6	Estimated close to 90% Jewish; median income $4,315; median rental $62.58; occupational structure upper-middle and upper class.
Ward 4 (precinct 35)	81	Estimated 71% Jewish; median rental $70.51; occupational structure upper middle and upper class.
Ward 29 (7 most Jewish precincts)	84.6	Estimated 69% Jewish; median income $3,900; occupational structure lower-middle and middle class.
Ward 48 (7 most Jewish precincts)	77.1	Estimated 62% Jewish; median income $3,699; median rental $70.67; occupational structure upper-middle and upper class.
Ward 46 (8 most Jewish precincts)	70.9	Estimated 62% Jewish; median income $3,756; median rental $61.86; occupational structure upper-middle and upper class.

FROM ROOSEVELT TO TRUMAN
TO STEVENSON

Jewish Democratic strength had to come down from its zenith in 1944. The surprising thing is that it diminished so little in 1948. Actually, the combined Truman-Wallace vote was almost as high in Jewish assembly districts and wards as the vote for F.D.R. had been four years before.

---

* Estimates of the relative Jewishness of these areas are drawn from an excellent population study by Erich Rosenthal, *The Jewish Population of Chicago, Size and Distribution as Derived From Voter Lists*, Chicago: Unpublished Ph.D. Thesis, University of Chicago, 1948.
   Income and rental figures were obtained from the 1950 Census for the city of Chicago. No median income figure was reported by the Department of Commerce for the census tract covering precinct 31, Ward 49. Nor was a median rental figure reported for the census tract covering the seven most Jewish precincts in Ward 29.

The Wallace vote was essentially a left-wing Democratic vote. In Ward 14 the Progressive candidate received 12 per cent of the vote, with a total of 87 per cent for Truman and Wallace combined. In Hartford's Wards 4 and 12 the Truman-Wallace vote was just three or four percentage points under the Roosevelt vote in '44. In the very Jewish Bronx 7th A.D. Wallace received 27 per cent of the vote. In the not quite as Jewish 2nd A.D. he won 21 per cent. The combined Truman-Wallace vote in the former area was nearly 90 per cent, in the latter over 80 per cent. The Democrats did lose ground, but they did not lose much of it to the Republicans. Even in precinct 8 in suburban Brookline nine per cent of the vote went to Wallace.

In 1952 a portion of every element of traditional Democratic strength except Negroes switched to Eisenhower. But analysis of returns from Jewish areas and the results of national surveys show that the Jewish defection was slight indeed. In many Jewish wards and assembly districts Stevenson maintained or increased the Truman percentage of the two-party vote. He matched it in the most Jewish precincts in Ward 14 in Pittsburgh, Ward 13 in Cincinnati, Wards 4 and 12 in Hartford, Wards 40 and 46 in Chicago, and almost maintained it in Ward 27 in Cleveland. He bettered it in Wards 12 and 14 in Boston, the most Jewish Assembly Districts in New York, and in Jewish precincts in Wards 24 and 4 in Chicago. Only in suburbs and in Southern cities were substantial inroads made on the Jewish Democratic vote in 1952.

FAITHFUL STILL

Fidelity to the Democratic Party in the Presidential elections of 1948 and 1952 was maintained by the Jews at a fairly high level. Despite the fact that the war was over, anti-Semitism had subsided, the survival of world Jewry was no longer an issue, and American Jews were prosperous, they voted for Truman or Wallace in 1948 and Stevenson in 1952. The issues which were important to most people in 1948 concerned the distribution of economic power.[11] Why did Jewish businessmen and professionals and tax-payers fail to line up with their occupational and economic interest groups? Both candidates were committed to Zionism. Both parties had adopted pro-Israel planks in their national platforms. There was even muttering in some Jewish communities that Truman had stalled too long before helping Israel, although many were grateful that he decided finally to recognize the new state. Some of Dewey's closest associates and advisors were Jews—Charles Breitel, his personal counsel, and Nathaniel Goldstein, his Attorney General, for example. There was no issue of foreign policy on which the two candidates clashed. Yet the Jews did not vote as other well-to-do Americans did. They held fast to the Democrats.

In 1952 the entire nation was swept off its feet by a great and pleasing professional soldier. The Republican candidate was a professed internationalist, President Eisenhower having distinguished himself in the war against Nazism as a benefactor of the Jews. There were many reasons why Jews might have been influenced by the pressures of their occupational and economic interest groups. Roosevelt had been dead seven years. Israel was no longer a partisan issue if it ever was. Both candidates were united in their opposition to Stalinism. Jews were disillusioned with the Wallace movement and other radical causes. The Republican nominee and the wing of the party which had nominated him accepted the main outlines of the New Deal. Candidate Eisenhower had little to say against the welfare state, only promised to run it more efficiently.

Why, then, did American Jews persist in voting for New Deal and Fair Deal candidates in 1948 and 1952?

---

11. Angus Campbell and Robert L. Kahn, *The People Elect a President* (Ann Arbor: Survey Research Center, University of Michigan, Institute for Social Research, 1952), p. 57.

CHAPTER VI

Presidential Choice in 1952

WHY DID about 75 per cent of American Jewry remain Democratic in 1952? What did most Jews see in the structure of two-party choice which other voters of similar socio-economic backgrounds failed to see? In order to answer these and related questions, a systematic sample of the voters in Boston's Ward 14 were interviewed by me and assistants working under my supervision. Of the 276 respondents interviewed, almost 84 per cent were Jewish. One hundred and ninety-nine, or 87 per cent of the eligible Jewish voters claimed to have cast ballots in 1952. Thirty-seven, or 79 per cent of the non-Jews said they voted. To assess the importance of various influences on these voters, questions were designed to produce responses which could be scaled by indices for socioeconomic status, political liberalism, and ethno-religious involvement. Census-type questions were also asked on age, sex, education, nationality background, etc. Another question was asked calling for an explanation of the vote. All questions were pretested.[1] Sixty-nine per cent of the 199 voting Jews, 54 per cent of the twenty-eight voting Catholics, and two of the eight voting Protestants reported having voted for Stevenson. Nonetheless, the Jews in the sample made more money, held better jobs, lived in better homes, and were about as well educated as the non-Jews.

---

1. Scalable questions were pretested on Brandeis University students. Other questions were pretested in a pilot survey of the parents of Brandeis students.

SOCIOECONOMIC STATUS AND THE
VOTE

Each respondent's socioeconomic status was computed by combining the scores for the answers to the income and occupational prestige questions, giving double weight to occupation. Non-Jews in the sample, as is always the case in national surveys, showed much greater Republican strength in the high SES groups than in the low groups. Quite the reverse was true for Jews, although differences in the Stevenson vote did not vary greatly from one SES group to another.

TABLE 3

DEMOCRATIC VOTE OF JEWS AND GENTILES BY
OCCUPATIONAL-INCOME STATUS, WARD 14

	% Democratic			
	Jews		Gentiles*	
Low SES	64 %	(36) †	60 %	(15)
Middle SES	66.3	(101)	41.7	(12)
High SES	72	(53)	30	(10)

The results for Jews in Ward 14 in 1952 are similar to those for Jews everywhere in 1940 and 1944, and appear to hold true for 1952 in the main sections of New York and Chicago. This is not to say that income and occupational prestige were not correlates of Eisenhower choice among Jews in some cities. In Cincinnati, where Jewish Ward 13 can be divided roughly into four tiers of precincts according to class status, the Eisenhower vote did rise sharply in the highest tier. But in Ward 14 that was not the case. It should be said that there are no extreme differences in wealth and occupational prestige in Ward 14. There were sixteen Jews in the sample who made more than $10,000 a year, and some streets, such as Wellington Hill St., are fine residential streets lined with well-kept one- and two-family homes, but the central living experiences of most Jews in the Ward are

* Though the total number of Gentiles is extremely small, the results will be reported for comparative purposes. Strikingly enough, the results nearly always parallel those found in national surveys.
† The figures in brackets will always signify the total number of any category voting.

similar. There, a prosperous lawyer may worship at the same synagogue as an unemployed plumber's helper. He may even be attended by the same doctor or eat at the same neighborhood restaurant, the C & G, located in the heart of the Ward on Blue Hill Avenue. If they live close to each other, they probably send their children to the same public school. The fact remains that the central living experiences of rich and poor Gentiles in Ward 14 are similar too; yet, vast differences exist between them in Democratic voting strength.

EDUCATION AND THE VOTE

There was a slight tendency for better educated Jews to prefer Eisenhower in 1952, but the pattern is hardly significant. In fact, the percentage of Jewish college graduates in Ward 14 voting for Stevenson was almost as high as for all Jews in the sample. The results for Gentiles support the accepted view that Republican choice is associated with high education among non-Jews.

TABLE 4

**DEMOCRATIC VOTE OF JEWS AND GENTILES
BY EDUCATIONAL GROUPS**

	% Democratic			
	Jews		*Gentiles*	
Some elementary school or less	79.5%	(39)	100 %	(1)
Elementary school grad	71.5	(21)	74	(4)
Some high school	73.9	(24)	66.6	(9)
High school grad	64.4	(62)	33.3	(9)
High school plus vocational or business school	53.4	(15)	0	(4)
Some college	64.3	(14)	20	(5)
College grad	68.3	(22)	60	(5)

AGE AND THE JEWISH VOTE

The results of other surveys reveal that when any group— Irish Catholics, Italians, Negroes—shift from their expected political predisposition, it is the younger voters who swing the most. Since the Jews did not shift their loyalties appreciably in 1952, there was little difference in the Democratic vote among Jewish age groups in Ward 14. On the other hand, the pronounced defection of Irish Catholic voters to Eisenhower was most noticeable among the younger voters.

TABLE 5

DEMOCRATIC VOTE OF JEWS AND GENTILES BY AGE GROUPS

	% Democratic			
Age Group	Jews		Gentiles	
21-34	70%	(53)	25%	(12)
34-54	63	(86)	50	(20)
54 plus	76	(54)	80	(5)

GENERATIONS AND THE VOTE

The distribution of the vote by age groups is not necessarily an index of voting preference by generations, although most first generation Jews are elderly and most third generation Hebrews tend to be young. As it turns out, there are too few third generation American Jews to tell just what the significance of generations might have been in 1952. In the first and second generation groups Stevenson strength was identical.

TABLE 6

DEMOCRATIC VOTE OF JEWS BY GENERATIONS*

	% Democratic	
First generation	67.5%	(80)
Second generation	67	(109)
Third generation	100	(8)

---

* The numbers for Gentiles are too small for fruitful comparison. Almost 50% of the Gentiles were third and fourth generation Americans.

A first generation American was defined as someone who was born in another country. A second generation American was someone who, though born in this country, had one or both parents born abroad. A third generation American as someone who had both parents born in this country, but had one or more grandparents born abroad.

Only 4.8% of the Jews were third generation Americans as compared to 48.6% of the Gentiles. Conversely, 43.8% of the Hebrews and only 13.1% of the Christians were first generation Americans.

NATIONALITY BACKGROUND AND THE VOTE

The backgrounds of West European and East European Jews differ in many important respects. First of all, West Europeans are largely products of the mid-nineteenth century immigration, while East Europeans are mainly of the last great immigration. In Germany and Austria, Jews centered in the cultural urban centers and were often leaders in the business world or in their professions. The Jews of Western Europe were a cultured and well-educated group. Many were highly assimilated to the ways of their countrymen.

From the villages of Poland and Russia came a different type of Jew. Religious orthodoxy prevailed. Illiteracy was high. Jews were cut off completely from political rights and from contact with the non-Jewish world. It has been customary to associate liberalism or radicalism in politics with the Jews from the East, not those from Germany and Austria-Hungary. Such an interpretation would lead one to predict that Eastern European Jews were much more Democratic than their coreligionists from the West. But this was not so in Ward 14 in 1952, as the scanty evidence below attests.

TABLE 7

DEMOCRATIC VOTE BY NATIONALITY BACKGROUND

Jews	% Democratic	
Russian and East European	68.3%	(173)
German and Austrian	80	(10)
Other	58.3	(12) *

ETHNO-RELIGIOUS INVOLVEMENT AND THE VOTE

From the unanimity of third generation Jews in approving of Stevenson, and from the fact that Jews from Western Europe were stronger for Stevenson than those from East of the Oder River, one might begin to suspect a paradox; that is, among Jews (heavily Democratic as a group) Jewishness

---

* These 12 breakdown as follows: 5 English (some of whom may actually be Russian or German); 3 Jews whose grandparents were born in this country; and 1 whose nationality background was undetermined.

itself correlates with a Republican choice. Quite logically, just the reverse should be true. If there is something about being a Jew that makes a man Democratic, the more Jewish he is the more likely he should be to vote Democratic. Actually, neither assumption can be supported by the facts. According to the results to questions designed to measure the depth of Jewish involvement of the respondents, there is scarcely any difference in the Stevenson vote between the orthodox, deep-feeling Jew and the well-assimilated Hebrew.

Separate questions were used to measure the depth of religious, cultural, and social Jewishness of respondents. The scores received in answer to each question were added to yield a total scalable ethno-religious involvement score. It was recognized that respondents might have commitments to Judaism which ran very deep, but which were psychological or intellectual and could not be measured by the EI scale.[2] For that reason all respondents were asked to pick three statements from a list (made originally in the pilot survey by respondents in answer to an open-end question) which best expressed what their religion meant to them.[3]

Stevenson voters made higher EI scores on the cultural and social Judaism tests, while Eisenhower voters scored slightly higher on the religious Judaism scale. The overall scores of each group were quite close, one-tenth of a point

2. For example, respondents would say, "Through being Jewish I find myself in sympathy for the underprivileged and oppressed." Or they would say simply, "I'm proud of being Jewish." Or "So much discrimination and anti-Semitism has made me feel that Judaism should not be a lost cause." These remarks all signify involvement, but the content of that involvement is not specific.

3. In the pilot survey of the parents and relatives of Brandeis college students the question was asked:

"What would you say being Jewish or Catholic or Protestant means to you?"

"Is it culture such as holidays and food, or your ideas about God, or ideas about what is right and wrong, or just what?"

Despite the fact that the question was structured so that answers with cultural, religious, and ethical content were favored, answers embodying such content accounted for only 50% of the 104 answers made. To many respondents, being Jewish was simply hereditary ("I was born Jewish and that's all"), or psychological ("Others think of me as a Jew"), or political ("I'm a strong Zionist").

separating them on a five point scale. From the results reproduced below it is not likely that differences in the vote could be attributed to differences in ethno-religious involvement, at least as measured by these scales.[4] Moreover, Eisenhower voters responded to the same kinds of statements in approximately the same distribution to express best what their religion meant to them.

TABLE 8

DEMOCRATIC VOTE OF JEWS BY ETHNIC INVOLVEMENT GROUPS

	% Democratic	
High EI	46.2%	(13)
High-Medium EI	72.4	(47)
Medium EI	69.5	(72)
Low-Medium EI	60.5	(43)
Low EI	80.1	(20)

---

4. It is entirely possible that the scales used were something less than a perfect measure of Jewishness. Eighteen questions were asked in all. For example, respondents were asked to rate the importance of such religious practices as saying prayers for dead parents. They were also asked to rate their approval or disapproval of such things as intermarriage, and to state whether or not they regularly read a Yiddish newspaper, kept a Kosher home, etc. While the results here show that Stevenson voters were just about as Jewish as Eisenhower voters, the findings in the 1948 Elmira study are different. (Bernard B. Berelson, Paul F. Lazarsfeld, and William N. McPhee, *Voting* [Chicago: University of Chicago Press, 1954], p. 72). The authors found that in Elmira, New York, those Jews who expressed a strong commitment to Judaism were more Democratic than those with low EI. The number of Jews involved was 108, less than half the number in the Boston survey, but a sizable group. However, certain subgroups are quite small. Those who neither attended services nor favored orthodox customs numbered only twelve. Still, the results may be quite sound. In Elmira in 1948, Jewish involvement may have correlated significantly with Democratic choice, while in Ward 14 no such correlation was forthcoming for 1952.

However, even in Elmira Republican choice may be less a function of low EI than a result of primary group contact with non-Jews. Probably both factors go somewhat together. Those Jews with low EI probably go to non-Jewish neighborhoods to live and participate in non-Jewish groups of various kinds. Those who for one reason or another have frequent contact wtih non-Jews probably become less orthodox as a result. If both results are correct, Elmira Jews must be different from Ward 14 Jews in some important respect. It is likely that the difference lies in the sheer concentration of Ward 14 Jews. Outside of sociological enclaves such as Ward 14, the EI scale used here might well be a significant separator of Republicans and Democrats.

The distribution of the Jewish vote by various demographic characteristics offers no clue to explain the continued
Democratic strength of Jews in the face of the Eisenhower
landslide. Nor do the results presented thus far suggest what
it was that prompted the Jewish minority to vote for the
President. It was not the poorer Jews, the older Jews, the
East European Jews, or even the more Jewish Jews who
preferred the Governor.

THE JEWISH RESPONSE TO STEVENSON

What did Jews perceive in Stevenson and the Democratic
Party in 1952 which made them vote for Stevenson, apparently without regard to differences in their socioeconomic
or religious characteristics? It was hoped that the answer to
that question would be forthcoming in the results to three
questions placed in the interview schedule. One question
was designed to test the political liberalism of respondents.
This particular test was aimed at discovering the basic attitudes of respondents toward the use of power. The criteria
on which the liberalism index was based were (1) a disposition to share power with out-groups and (2) a disposition to respect those who are different. It may well be
that these criteria define political altruism and not liberalism
as it is commonly understood. Whether the question yields
an altruism or liberalism index is not important here. The
results show that there was considerable difference between
the Gentile and Jewish respondents in Ward 14. After the
answers were scaled, respondents were divided into six
categories ranging from very strong liberals to very strong
illiberals. While 40 per cent of the Jews qualified as political
liberals or altruists, only 26 per cent of the Gentiles did so.
The results were not surprising in the light of reports on
other liberalism-conservatism tests. No matter what criteria
have been used to define liberalism and conservatism, Jews
have invariably been rated more liberal than Christians!

Did Jews perceive liberalism in Stevenson and the Democratic Party? All Stevenson voters were asked to pick three statements from a list (all statements were originally made by respondents in answer to an open-end question in the pilot survey) which best expressed why they preferred Stevenson. They were also asked to choose two statements from another list which best expressed what they liked least about Eisenhower.

To a much greater extent than the Christians, the Jews in the sample emphasized the personal qualifications and liberalism of Stevenson and/or the Democratic Party. Gentiles tended to stress the fact that the Democrats and/or Stevenson favored their own economic group while Eisenhower and the Republicans did not.

The results to these questions hardly prove that it was the political liberalism of the Jews which kept them Democratic in 1952, but the evidence such as it is, taken together with the findings of Mr. Louis Harris of the Elmo Roper organization,[5] suggests that Jews did tend to think of Mr. Stevenson as the more "liberal" candidate and the Democratic Party as the "liberal" party.

LIBERALISM AND THE STEVENSON-EISENHOWER CHOICE

If, as suggested, it was the liberalism of the Jews which oriented them toward a Democratic choice, it might be supposed that those Jews who were least liberal were the Eisenhower voters. Although it is true that a higher proportion of liberal or politically altruistic Jews voted for Stevenson than voted for him in the moderate or illiberal groups, the total number of liberals is quite small, and the differences between groups are not large.

---

5. Louis Harris, *Is There a Republican Majority?* (Harper & Brothers, New York: 1954), pp. 161-163. Harris found that Jews by a better than two-to-one count thought Stevenson would really do something about civil rights; by a four-to-three count they thought Ike would not.

TABLE 9

DEMOCRATIC VOTE OF JEWS AND GENTILES BY LIBERALISM GROUPS

	% Democratic			
	Jews		*Gentiles*	
Liberals (altruists)	87.5%	(25)	50 %	(4)
Moderates	67	(124)	52.3	(24)
Illiberals	64.5	(43)	38.9	(9)

It is entirely possible that the overwhelming disposition of the Jews to vote Democratic in recent decades is a function of their liberalism, but it is also possible that Jewish votes for Eisenhower were something other than a manifestation of illiberalism. Literally dozens of Jewish voters indicated in their replies to open-end questions that they thought Eisenhower was a liberal himself.

For a satisfactory explanation of the slight Jewish Democratic defection in 1952, it is probably well to start with the proposition that some Jews were bound to be affected by the factors which caused the Eisenhower landslide in the nation at large. But which Jews were influenced and which were not? It was not necessarily the rich Jews, or the well-educated, or the third generation Jews, or those less ethnically involved, or the younger Jews who showed disproportionate Eisenhower strength. Such evidence as is available strongly suggests that the Republican vote went up among those Jews who had the most frequent and extensive contact with non-Jews in primary groups. While it is not possible to prove this hypothesis quantitatively with the results of the Ward 14 survey (the appropriate questions were never asked), inferences can be drawn from some of these results and from a further discussion of aggregate returns.

Three sets of data tend to support this notion: first, the difference in the Stevenson vote between men and women in Ward 14; second, the results of election surveys in Jewish colleges; and third, the election results for Jewish suburban areas compared to those for metropolitan centers.

JEWISH MEN AND WOMEN IN THE 1952 ELECTION

Although the Survey Research Center reported that about the same proportion of males and females in the nation as a whole voted for Eisenhower,[6] the results of the sample survey in Ward 14 show that 83.3 per cent of the Jewish women voters preferred Stevenson as compared to only 59.4 per cent of the men.[7] To be sure, the results of national surveys in the past have shown Jewish women to be somewhat more Democratic than Jewish men, but the differences between them were three or four per cent and not 24 per cent.[8] Keeping in mind the possibility of sampling and reporting bias, the results still appear to defy explanation until consideration is given to the importance of primary group contacts in the formulation of electoral decision.

Most students of electoral behavior emphasize the importance of face-to-face contacts in the shaping of vote choice.[9] The evidence from the Ward 14 survey indicates that the large difference in the male-female vote for Stevenson can be explained by the fact that Jewish women in Ward 14 have very little contact with non-Jews in primary

---

6. Angus Campbell, Gerald Gurin, and Warren E. Miller, *The Voter Decides;* (Evanston: Row, Peterson & Co., 1954), p. 170. Harris, *op. cit.,* Chapter VII, found women were generally more attracted to Eisenhower than the men.

7. There was only a difference of 2% between the Gentile male and female voters in the sample.

8. Bower, *op. cit.,* p. 11.
Korchin, *op. cit.,* p. 97.

9. Paul F. Lazarsfeld, Bernard Berelson, and Hazel Gaudet, *The People's Choice* (New York: Columbia University Press, 1948), Chapter XVI. Campbell, Gurin, and Miller, *op. cit.,* pp. 199-206.

Even though Lazarsfeld was preoccupied with asserting the relationship between demographic factors and the vote, he emphasized that it was the interpersonal influence within the small group which was most important.

groups, but their husbands, fathers, and sons are thrust into such groups fairly often.

Most of the women rarely leave the ward itself. Their contacts are almost exclusively limited to the immediate family and neighborhood. One young woman told the writer that she never met a Protestant until she went to college. For the most part, Jewish women in Ward 14 talked to other Jewish women during the election campaign in 1952. On the other hand, many of the men from Ward 14 work outside of the area, and were thereby exposed (in Lazarsfeld's phrase) to "cross-pressures" in mixed work and friendship groups.

In 1952 the Jewish group as a group held fast to its Democratic moorings while the nation, for many reasons, swung to Eisenhower. While Jewish men were exposed to the opinions of friends at the work bench, customers in the store, clients in the office and so on, Jewish women were insulated from these cross-pressures to a considerable extent.

What evidence is there to support such a view? If the men were exposed to cross-pressures directly, these pressures were presumably filtered through them to their wives and mothers. There is evidence that some Eisenhower voters did try to influence their wives' votes, and in at least two cases succeeded. One young housewife, whose husband was an electrical appliance salesman for a non-Jewish firm, volunteered at the end of her interview, "I was for Stevenson until the last minute when my husband made me change my mind. He felt it was time for a change, and then I thought maybe Eisenhower would end the Korean War." Another middle-aged woman was married to a sales executive at Jordan Marsh. "The only Jew in his department," she volunteered. Throughout the campaign he tried to persuade her to switch to Eisenhower without success until she entered the voting booth. As she recalled, "I told him that morning that I would vote for Stevenson. But then I changed. I don't know why."

In both cases the husbands for Eisenhower were men

who were in frequent and sustained contact with non-Jews in their primary work groups. Both families were well-educated, the kind in which political opinions of wives and husbands are likely to be exchanged. It is probable that most of the housewives in the sample were not as exposed to non-Jewish or Republican influences as much as these two.[10]

One twenty-eight-year-old chemical engineer in frequent contact with non-Jews and high on the liberalism scale, who had voted for Truman in 1948, showed the effect of non-Jewish primary group influences in voting for Eisenhower. He explained, "I voted for him (Ike) despite his campaign which was sad. Stevenson was the better man. Eisenhower just talked in generalities and promised everything, but *everyone said* there was too much corruption in the federal government, and it's good to turn those fellows out."

There is one additional check on this primary group explanation for the disparity in the male-female vote. Some of the women were working women. Presumably they would be in greater contact with non-Jews and Republican cross-pressures. Such contact would be reflected in the vote. While only 70 per cent of the working and single women in the Ward 14 sample voted for Stevenson, 84 per cent of the housewives chose the Governor.

Though Jewish men had many more non-Jewish primary group contacts than Jewish women in previous elections, the disparity in Democratic vote between them was not so great because (1) the non-Jewish world was also a Democratic

10. Incredible as the disparity between the male and female Stevenson vote appears to be, a check back to a breakdown of the vote in the pilot mail survey of Brandeis college parents and relatives show the results in the pilot project to be similar to those for Ward 14 to an amazing degree. In the pilot survey fifty-nine Jewish respondents voted in 1952. Of the thirty-three men, only twenty-three said they chose Stevenson (69.8%). Of the 26 voting women, twenty-four replied that they voted for Stevenson (92.3%), an amazing difference of 22.5%, almost identical to the difference in the Ward 14 sample. Of course, confidence limits could not be applied in such a survey, but the sample was cross-sectional for America's upper-middle-class Jewry.

world; and more importantly, (2) Jewish solidarity in regard to the political issues of the 1940 and 1944 campaigns especially was so strong that Jewish men as well as women were almost impervious to outside influences.

There may be other reasons for the stronger female response to Stevenson. There is some evidence from the survey results that they were slightly more disturbed than the men because Eisenhower was a military man and that Stevenson's urbane and learned manner were more pleasing to the Jewish women than to the men, but evidence available is shadowy at best.

JEWISH COLLEGE COMMUNITIES AND THE 1952 ELECTION

At least suggestive of the importance of immediate group contacts on the Jewish vote in 1952 are the results of polls taken at Yeshiva College and Brandeis University. At Yeshiva, a school which is 100 per cent Jewish, Eisenhower received a mere four per cent of the vote. Brandeis is a nonsectarian, Jewish-sponsored school. Probably as much as ten per cent of its student body is not Jewish.[11] In the Brandeis poll Stevenson received 88 per cent of the vote.

The Brandeis students represent a cross-section of American Jewry—religious, irreligious, urban, small town, suburban, poor, well-to-do. Yet the Brandeis vote, including non-Jews, was 14 per cent higher than that reported for the national Jewish population by survey organizations and ten per cent higher than that reported for a sample of fifty-nine of their own parents and relatives questioned by mail in a pilot survey. Jewish students came to Brandeis and Yeshiva with strong Democratic leanings. Finding their own opinions almost unanimously reinforced in student face-to-face groups, there were few defections. At home their parents were ex-

---

11. Of course, it is impossible to know just how many non-Jews there are at Brandeis. While the percentage is growing all the time, the percentage quoted here is probably correct within five per cent for 1952.

posed to more frequent and numerous contact with non-Jews in Republican-oriented groups.

SUBURBAN JEWRY AND THE 1952 ELECTION

It has already been seen that Jewish wards and assembly districts in the very large cities showed little Democratic loss from 1948. If national survey results are correct, and it must be assumed they are within the confidence limits assigned, it is reasonable to conclude that what Democratic losses there were occurred among those Jews who are dispersed in Gentile areas or in the suburbs. The votes of the former cannot be reported, since they are buried in the aggregate returns for non-Jewish wards. But simple arithmetic does suggest that defections took place in just such cases. Moreover, the returns from suburban Jewish areas support the hypothesis outlined here on the influence of primary group contacts on Jewish voting choice in 1952. Reports from Westchester and Long Island in New York and from Brookline and Newton near Boston indicate that Jews in the suburbs were primarily responsible for the Jewish defections which did take place.

Although Jews may cluster together even in the tree-lined neighborhoods and country clubs of the suburbs, they are exposed to much greater non-Jewish face-to-face contact than are the Hebrews of Ward 14 or the Bronx. Jewish families in the suburbs participate in community affairs. Both the men and the women meet their non-Jewish neighbors in primary groups. They discover a common interest in the tax rate or the problems of the high school, perhaps one-third Jewish. Their interest in the local synagogue or Jewish community center may be more lively than it ever was back in Brooklyn, but their associations are no longer so preponderantly Jewish.

In 1944, suburban Jewry was hardly less Democratic than its coreligionists in the city because Jewish group involvement in the outcome of the election was so high. Even in precinct 8 in suburban Brookline, F.D.R. received 79 per cent of the vote. In 1952 the Democratic vote there slipped to 52 per cent of the total. Brookline is a bedroom area to Boston. Its voters were subjected to cross-pressures in primary groups which even many of the well-to-do in Dorchester and Mattapan did not experience, and in 1952 those pressures were greatest in the suburbs where the Eisenhower plurality was largest.

CHAPTER VII

The Democrats and the Jews

MORE IMPORTANT than the causes of Democratic defection among Jews in 1952 are the causes of persistent Democratic attachment over the last three decades. American Jewry would have elected the Democratic candidate in 1952 by a much greater landslide than the one that actually swept the Democrats out of office. This, despite the fact that they are as well paid, fed, and educated as the most successful Republican denominational groups. To understand Jewish fidelity to the Democrats in 1948 and 1952, it is necessary to go back to Franklin Roosevelt and the complete devotion which American Israelites felt for the scion of Hyde Park and the causes he championed.

THE ROOSEVELT APPEAL

The synagogues were more crowded after Franklin Roosevelt's death than they had been for a long time. None felt a greater sense of loss and grief than America's Jews. No group had been so devoted to him during his lifetime. Jews were drawn to him as to a magnet. So numerous were his Jewish friends and advisors that the slogan "Jew Deal" became popular in anti-Semitic circles. He appointed his Dutchess County friend and neighbor, Henry Morgenthau, Jr., Secretary of the Treasury, the second Jew to hold a cabinet post. Herbert Lehman, Samuel Rosenman, Sam Cohen, Felix Frankfurter, David Lilienthal, Bernard Baruch, Anna Rosenberg, Sidney Hillman, and David Niles were all close to him at one time or another. As the editor of one Jewish periodical wrote shortly after Roosevelt's passing, "We Jews have always felt particularly close to Roosevelt. He understood us. . . ."[1]

Other Presidents before F.D.R. had laid cornerstones for synagogues, made public addresses before Jewish organizations, and had repeatedly attacked anti-Semitism, but only of Roosevelt could the Jews say, "He understood us." When he died, disbelief seized the Jewish community. In the pulpits Rabbis actually compared him to Moses. The *Hartford Jewish Ledger* recorded, "We loved him. He has found a place in the annals of Jewish history even as his name will go ringing down the ages as one of the prophets of a new day. A well-known Rabbi exclaimed, ". . . for the people of Israel he was the luminous center about which gathered all yearning for justice, our hope for a better world, all aspirations of good and just men everywhere."[2]

Is it possible to understand fully the amazing appeal which this highly born Episcopalian had for American Jewry?

The two broad political triumphs which history will associate with the name of Franklin Roosevelt were: first, leading the American nation into European and international affairs on behalf of the allies against the fascists and Nazis in World War II; and second, persuading the nation to accept the proposition that the national government is responsible for the welfare of all its citizens. In our time the first has gone under the name of internationalism and the second under the name of liberalism. In both political adventures Roosevelt had the almost solid support of American Jewry.

JEWISH INTERNATIONALISM

During the late thirties there was no stronger interventionist group in the United States than the Jews. If the Jews

---

1. Max Kleinman, *Synagogue Tributes* (New York: Bloch Publishing Co., 1946), p. 237.
2. *Ibid.,* p. 54.

had never before or would never again show an interest in
internationalism, the survival of world Jewry itself made
such a course mandatory in the 1930's and 1940's. Roosevelt
began a series of public protests in 1935 against anti-Semitism
in Germany and was the political leader of the interventionist forces in this country. How could Jews help but be drawn
to the man most likely to induce American public opinion
to recognize the need for an active American role in European affairs? It is easy to see how the internationalist group
interest of the Jews prompted them to turn in thumping
90 per cent majorities for Roosevelt in 1940 and 1944, but
the survival of world Jewry was no longer at stake in the
1948 and 1952 elections. Yet, American Jews continued
to vote for the candidates of the Party which took the inter-
ventionist-internationalist stand in the late 1930's and early
1940's.

Recent studies show that Jewish support for internationalism persisted long after the defeat of Hitler. Survey
results in recent years reveal that Jews have been first among
the supporters for the U.N., world government plans, Point
Four, more liberal immigration policies, and aid to Europe.
In survey results for *Time* magazine analyzed by Haveman
and West, Jewish and Gentile college graduates were asked
an "internationalism-isolationism" question. Agreement with
five of the six following statements was indexed as internationalism:

1. The United Nations should have the right to
make conclusions that would bind members to a course
of action;

2. It is not true that if we allow more immigrants
to this country we will lower our standard of culture;

3. It is not true that if we lower our tariffs to permit
more foreign goods in this country we will lower our
standard of living;

4. Over the next decade we must try to make the
standard of living in the rest of the world rise more
rapidly than in our own country;

5. It is not true that deep ideological differences between countries are irreconcilable;

6. This statement is untrue: We are not likely to have lasting peace until the United States and its allies are stronger than all other countries.[3]

Agreement with these statements, an excellent index of internationalism in 1948 when the question was asked, was forthcoming from Jewish graduates twice as often as from non-Jews. Sixty-four per cent of the Jews were indexed as internationalists, five per cent as isolationists; 34 per cent of the Catholics were called internationalists, 20 per cent isolationists; 39 per cent of the Protestants were internationalists, 19 per cent isolationists.

Did Jews perceive that their group interest in internationalism would best be served by the election of Truman or Henry Wallace? Presumably the answer is yes. Otherwise, how could the extraordinary defection to Henry Wallace be accounted for? Wallace based much of his campaign on the failure of Truman to carry on the internationalism of Roosevelt (negotiation with Russia) while the Republicans, if they debated foreign policy at all, chided Truman for being too internationalist.[4]

What of 1952? Does Jewish internationalism persist even now? In the Ward 14 survey conducted in 1952 the following question was asked:

Please say whether you agree or disagree with the following statements.

1. In matters of foreign policy the United States should try to make decisions in the United Nations and not make decisions by itself.

2. The United States should tax its citizens to spend money in parts of Asia and Africa to help raise standards of living in those countries.

3. Haveman and West, *op. cit.,* pp. 100-101.
4. Wallace must have also won some votes for his strong pro-Zionist stand.

Almost 78 per cent of the Jews in the sample were in agreement with the first statement, 23 per cent of these in strong agreement. Sixty-nine per cent of the Gentiles were in agreement, only 13.4 per cent of these in strong agreement. Forty-four and one-half per cent of the Jews agreed to the second statement, ten per cent in strong agreement. Only 28.4 per cent of the Christians agreed, not one of these in strong agreement. Later, in 1953, the Elmo Roper organization asked the American people what their attitudes were on the United Nations. While 58 per cent of the Jews in the sample desired a stronger U.N. or even world government, only 48 per cent of the Protestants and 42 per cent of the Catholics agreed.[5]

National Roper surveys also showed that the issues of foreign policy were of first importance to the Jews. They were one of the few groups not critical of our Korean policy, and which favored negotiation there. Jews favored the European aid program more enthusiastically than Gentiles did.[6] These attitudes on foreign affairs were more in tune with what Stevenson was saying than with Eisenhower's veiled criticisms of Yalta. American Jews continued to associate their own group interest in internationalism with the fortunes of the Democratic Party in Presidential elections.

ECONOMIC LIBERALS: TWENTIETH-CENTURY STYLE

The Jews were strong in their support for Franklin Roosevelt's belief that the national government ought to assume the responsibility for the welfare of all Americans. They have been foremost in their support for social security, unemployment insurance, favorable labor legislation, and progressive taxation. They have been economic liberals, in the American twentieth-century use of the term, tending

---

5. Elmo Roper, "American Attitudes on International Organization," *Public Opinion Quarterly* (Winter, 1953), p. 410.

6. Louis Harris, *op. cit.*, p. 161.

always to favor the lower income groups in their opinions on the distribution of economic power.

In 1936 and 1932 particularly, such views made obvious economic sense to many Jews themselves. Russian Jews coming to this country at the turn of the century were among our poorest immigrants, bringing less cash per capita with them than the Irish, the Germans, the Scotch, the Scandinavians, the Portuguese, and the Northern Italians. Many struggled to some kind of success in small business or the entertainment world during the twenties. A few succeeded in the professions, but the Jews, like other Americans of recent immigrant stock, felt the cruel blows of the depression and were surely grateful for Roosevelt's efforts to loosen the grip of poverty. One eighty-year-old resident of Ward 14, a lifelong registered Republican, who voted for Eisenhower in 1952, recalled during his interview, "I voted for Roosevelt every time. I blessed him every day. He done a good turn for everybody. Years ago people panhandled, their shoes were tied up with wire, and they didn't have enough [money] to get a shave. After Roosevelt old people go around clean and with a shave."

But as the sons and daughters of illiterate Jews from Boston's old West End or New York's lower East Side graduated from college and went into the professions and white collar jobs, and as business conditions became more favorable for the small Jewish merchants, American Jews began to climb the economic class ladder. By 1940 and 1944, and even in 1936, Jews alone among ethno-religious groups did not vote their pocketbooks.

American Jews tended to agree with the position of the Democratic Party that labor unions should have a good deal of power and that the federal government should guarantee economic security to its citizens. In 1944 the American Institute of Public Opinion asked several national samples the following question.

Which of these statements do you most agree with?

1. The most important job for the government is to make certain that there are good opportunities for each person to get ahead on his own;

2. The most important job for the government is to guarantee every person a decent and steady job and standard of living.

When Beverly and Wesley Allinsmith analyzed the results for religious denominations they found high occupational status correlated with agreement to statement 1 for every denominational group but the Jews. The results showed that 53.8 per cent of the Jewish business and professional men were for government guarantees, more than twice the average proportion for non-Jews in those same occupations. Jewish white collar workers were considerably more for government guarantees than Christian white collar workers in all denominations, and Jewish manual workers were more for government guarantees than all others but Baptist manual workers.[7] Moreover, there were proportionately fewer Jewish manual workers than in any other denomination—only 26.8 per cent as compared to 54.7 per cent for the Catholics or 51.4 per cent for the Baptists, the low status groups. Yet, a higher proportion of Jews than any other group answered the first part of the following question affirmatively when it was asked in Gallup polls:

Would you agree that everybody would be happier, more secure and more prosperous if working people were given more power and influence in government, or would you say that we all would be better off if working people had no more power than they had now.[8]

Although 58.8 per cent of the Jews wanted to give more power to working people, only 31 per cent of the Congre-

7. Allinsmith, *op. cit.*, p. 379.
8. *Ibid.*

gationalists, 37.1 per cent of the Presbyterians, and 34.7 per cent of the Episcopalians—the other high occupational status groups—agreed.[9]

In 1948, Haveman and West also examined the answers of college students to a question on the role of government in American society. If a respondent disagreed with two of the following statements he was indexed as being pro-New Deal.[10]

> 1. Democracy depends fundamentally upon the existence of free enterprise;
> 2. The best government is the one which governs least;
> 3. Government planning should be strictly limited for it almost invariably results in the loss of essential liberties and freedom;
> 4. Individual liberty and justice under law is not possible in Socialist countries.

Although the Jewish college graduates were making more money in better jobs than their Catholic and Protestant peers, only 34 per cent of the Protestants and 39 per cent of the Catholics were pro-New Deal compared to 66 per cent of the Jewish graduates.[11]

In the Ward 14 survey, respondents were asked one question dealing with economic liberalism and the role of the

---

9. There are two ancillary factors which influence Jewish business and professional men away from "rugged individualism." The desire of Jewish businessmen to achieve governmental guarantees may result partly from the fact that they are in the most individualistic and competitive of all businesses—the garment, fur, and retail trades. Although consolidation is increasingly the rule in the non-Jewish industrial world, Jewish industries are highly competitive. In an economic market which finds other industries increasingly concentrated, some Jewish businessmen may welcome the regulation of those industries.

Another factor affecting the attitude of Jews of high occupational status towards government guarantees and labor is that Jewish families tend to be more organic than Christian families. Almost every successful businessman or lawyer has a less fortunate brother or father or uncle living in the same city, often in the same house.

10. Haveman and West, *op. cit.*, pp. 98-99.

11. *Ibid.*, p. 192.

federal government in promoting national welfare. They were asked to say whether they agreed or disagreed with the following statement:

> It is fair for those of us in Massachusetts who have bigger incomes than the people in Kentucky to help pay for their roads, better education, and things like that.

While 56.7 per cent of the Jewish respondents agreed, 14.2 per cent in strong agreement, only 39.8 per cent of the Christians in the sample did likewise, with a mere 4.5 per cent in strong agreement.

The results of all of these studies show American Jews to be economic liberals—twentieth-century style—almost without regard to differences in class lines within the group, and despite the fact that Jews as a group now are perched near if not on the top of the economic class ladder.

In foreign policy matters the Jews have been internationalists. In economic policy matters they have been "liberals" in the New Deal sense of the word. To the extent that the internationalist-isolationist fight and the liberal-conservative struggle in national politics has been dichotomized between the Democrats and Republicans, Jews have been drawn back to the party of Jefferson. On these two broad issues the main battle lines were drawn during the 1930's. To some extent it is the memory of those battles over which Democrats and Republicans fight today. To some extent the battle is still real, although the lines are often fuzzy.

NEW ISSUES: NEGRO RIGHTS AND FREEDOM
OF THE MIND

Since the death of Roosevelt two new major political issues have divided Americans. Each of these is really a cluster of issues. One deals with Negro rights and the other with freedom of the mind. When President Truman made an issue of the federal FEPC and other recommendations of his Commission on Civil Rights, he found enthusiastic supporters among Jews. Samuel Lubell discovered there was no group in 1948 stronger for FEPC measure than the Jews.[12] In the East Bronx he found Jewish community leaders desperately trying to work out problems with newly arrived Negroes and Puerto Ricans.[13] Again, in 1952 the results of surveys on the Negro rights issue showed that Jews were zealous in the quest for legislation protecting those rights and that they thought Democrats could do more about accomplishing such legislation than Republicans.[14] Even in the South, equality for the Negro is espoused more readily by the Jews than by their neighbors. The Wallace movement in 1948 received its strongest support from Jews in Atlanta, one of the few Southern cities where it amounted to anything at all. More than seven out of every ten Jews in the city of Roanoke, Virginia, favor the 1954 Supreme Court desegregation decision, according to a mail survey of Jewish adults in that city.[15] No less than 82 per cent of the Stevenson voters in the Roanoke sample approved of desegregation in the public schools as compared to 55 per cent of the Eisenhower voters. The Roanoke Jews as well as others generally share the belief that Democratic Presidents will do more for the Negroes than would Republicans in the White House. Among the Roanoke respondents who strongly approved of desegregation 70 per cent voted for Stevenson compared to only 20 per cent of those who strongly disapproved.

The other issue which has recently agitated and divided Americans, while here labeled "freedom of the mind," is really a bundle of things packaged in one. It is the issue of communism in government, the rights and wrongs of Congressional investigating committees, the federal security program, the enforcement of sedition legislation, the use of high

12. Samuel Lubell, *The Future of American Politics* (New York: Harper & Brothers, 1952) , pp. 96-97.

13. *Ibid.,* pp. 88-89.

14. Harris, *op. cit.,* p. 162.

15. Almost every adult Jew in the city of Roanoke was questioned by mail. A total of 171 replies were forthcoming, more than one-third of the entire adult Jewish population.

position to make reckless and unsubstantiated charges, etc. According to 1952 surveys on these civil liberties issues, the Jews were at variance with every other segment of the population. More than any other group, the Jews defended the rights of nonconformists. More than any other group, they were shocked at the behavior of Senator McCarthy. Only the Jews thought that McCarthy handled the issue of communists in government more poorly than the State Department, President Truman, and the rest of Congress combined. Every Roper and Gallup public opinion poll has shown the Jews to be overwhelmingly hostile to McCarthy, although a majority of Christians viewed him with favor at the height of his power. The reaction of Jews to the charges of Nixon, McCarthy, and Jenner that the Democratic administration had been honeycombed with communists was distinctly negative.

On all these issues, according to the Roper results, the Jews "found something of a champion in Stevenson."[16] They had come to identify national Democratic administrations since Roosevelt with their own group interests in internationalism and liberalism. Now two other liberalism-conservatism issues emerged to fortify their Democratic predispositions. On the first, Harry Truman waged a vigorous campaign for Negro rights. On the second, McCarthy, Nixon, and Jenner, hung like albatrosses around the neck of the General while Stevenson defended intellectual independence and "the right to be unpopular" as hallmarks of civilization.

The Jews are interested in the things which the Democratic Presidential candidates have urged on the nation. Whether the Jews are liberals on economic questions, Negro rights, and civil liberties because of their own self-interest or because of altruism or a combination of both, liberals they are.

How explicitly do Jews identify their own group interests with the fortunes of the Democratic Party? The results of

---

16. Harris, *op. cit.*, p. 163.

one question asked in a pilot survey of Brandeis students' parents suggests an answer. Respondents were asked the following question:

> What are some of the reasons you voted for the candidate you did vote for in the Presidential election?
> a. For example, do you think one party represents the underdog more than the other?
> b. Do you think one party tends to be more fair-minded and less selfish than the other?
> c. Do you think one party is better for your religious group than the other?

There were fifty-nine Jewish voters in the sample, of which forty-seven voted for Stevenson.[17] With few exceptions these believed the Democrats represented the underdog more and were more fair-minded and less selfish than the Republicans. Even some of the Eisenhower voters agreed to those propositions, but thought "it was time for a change" or that "corruption ought to be rooted out of government." Of the fifty-nine respondents, only thirty-five would venture to comment on the last question at all.

While 40 per cent of the respondents who answered the question felt Democrats were or are better for Jews in some manner, none suggested that the Republicans were or are better for their group. The results are all the more surprising because of the usual unwillingness of persons to make explicit their feelings about the relationship of their political to their religious preferences. Twenty-four of the fifty-nine respondents ducked the question altogether. Were William Howard Taft alive he would shake his head in disbelief. Paraphrasing Isaiah he might ask, "Since when have the faithful Jews gone over to the Democrats?" Hardly could he say in 1954 what he said less than forty years ago—that the Jews make the best Republicans.

---

17. This 80 per cent Stevenson vote is from a group whose average family income was $6,500.

TABLE 10

HOW JEWS VIEW THE MAJOR PARTIES

Answer	No.
The Democrats are better for the Jews	7
The Democrats used to be better for the Jews but no difference now	3
The Democrats were better for the Jews under Roosevelt, "but Willkie would have been good too"	1
When the Democrats are in power more Jews are in administrative positions	1
There are more anti-Semites in the Republican Party	1
Others say the Democrats are better for the Jews	1
Total	**14**
The Republicans are better for the Jews	0
Neither party is better or worse for the Jews	20
Unsure which is better	1
Not answering	24
Total	**59**

WHAT NEXT?

Will Jews persist in their Democratic attachment or will they vote their pocketbooks in 1956? They were predominantly Republican not long ago; can the Republicans enlist their support again? Many Jews perceive President Eisenhower as a liberal. Although few in number, some strongly liberal Jewish Republicans have joined his administration and are trying to remake the Grand Old Party in the image of Abraham Lincoln. The head of the President's cabinet secretariat, Maxwell Rabb, has tried to picture Eisenhower as a liberal. The President's first Solicitor General, Simon Sobeloff, selected by Eisenhower as a Circuit Court Judge in 1955, may well have been the most liberal Solicitor General in history. It was Sobeloff who proposed that the government make a confession of error in the case of Dr. John Peters, fired under the old Truman loyalty program as a federal health consultant. This was the first public break by a Solicitor General with his superiors on a major policy question in decades. Sobeloff also takes a more liberal view on immigration and other issues than the one usually professed by leaders of the administration. Another pro-Eisenhower Jew who has caught public fancy is liberal Jacob Javits, elected Attorney General of New York State in 1954 despite the Democratic sweep there.

There are many non-Jews who also want to make the Republican Party "the liberal party." Theodore McKeldin, former Mayor of Baltimore, now Governor of Maryland, has advanced liberal views on civil liberties and social and economic questions which have been popular with the Jews in his state. Senators James Duff of Pennsylvania, Clifford P. Case of New Jersey, and Leverett Saltonstall of Massachusetts are well liked by the Jews in their respective states. The wing of the Party which these men and the President represent is pledged to expand efforts in international organization and social democracy initiated by F.D.R. If this wing, by some miracle, were able to dominate completely the national Republican convention in 1956, Jewish voters would unquestionably be more favorably disposed to the G.O.P.

Election results in Jewish districts since 1952 indicate, however, that liberal Republicans have not made their case with Hebrew voters. If anything, Democrats seem to have recouped slight losses in those areas, and strong liberal Republicans have been beaten badly by New Deal Democrats. Jews have continued to vote Democratic far out of proportion to their numbers and much beyond what is expected of a group with a relatively high proportion of entrepreneurs, white collar, and professional workers.

If any Republican was expected to run well in Jewish districts it was Senator Clifford Case in 1954. A devoted champion of civil liberties, liberal in economic matters, and a firm internationalist, Case is warmly received in Jewish communities in New Jersey. He had been a Republican maverick in the House of Representatives, voting with Fair Dealers more often than with the Republicans, and during the campaign he openly attacked Senator McCarthy. As an unequivocal Eisenhower Republican his campaign was a test of Eisenhower strength. Republican managers expected a strong vote for Case in Paterson's Ward 11, a spacious residential area, approximately 65 per cent Jewish. Despite his victory in the election, Senator Case received only 42.8 per cent of the ballots cast for Senator in Ward 11. Had he run against a conservative anti-Truman Democrat, Case might have swept the district. But his opponent was Charles P. Howell, a congressman with a firm New Deal and internationalist record. Case actually did not run as well as his more conservative senior Senatorial colleague, H. Alexander Smith, who won 48.2 per cent of the votes cast for Senator in Ward 11 in 1952. The turnout veered sharply downward in 1954, but there is no reason to suppose that Republicans stayed at home in larger numbers than Democrats. In 1953 the turnout for the New Jersey Gubernatorial contest was much higher than it had been in previous years, and the Democratic candidate, Robert Meyner, received 58.7 per cent of Ward 11's vote against Republican Paul L. Troast. Meyner's plurality was slightly higher than Howell's and 7.6 per cent greater than Stevenson's in 1952. Republicans have not made gains in this Jewish upper-middle-class suburban area since 1952. Just the reverse has been true. While probably as many as six out of ten Jews in Ward 11 voted for Stevenson in 1952, nearly seven out of ten voted for Meyner in 1953 and Howell in 1954.

When pitted against liberal Democratic opponents, liberal Republicans have not fared well in other Jewish areas. Massachusetts' Senator Leverett Saltonstall, as will be shown later in more detail, has always been favored with a large share of Jewish votes. He has established a reputation in the Jewish community of Boston for honesty, fair-mindedness, and liberalism. Like Case, Saltonstall stressed his support of Eisenhower in his quest for re-election in 1954. His response to almost every difficult question was that he backed the Eisenhower record. Democratic opponent Foster Furculo ran a quiet campaign based largely on his reputation as a liberal in Congress where he represented Springfield. The Saltonstall vote was the lowest the Senator ever received in Ward 14. In his Senatorial campaigns in 1944 and 1948 he received 41 and 32.3 per cent of the vote, respectively. In 1954 only 29.5 per cent of the ballots cast in Ward 14 were for Saltonstall.

Saltonstall's Senatorial colleague Irving M. Ives of New York is another liberal Republican who ran on the Eisenhower record in 1954. Author of a bill to outlaw discrimination in employment in New York State, Ives has achieved a pro-labor and internationalist record in the United States Senate. As far as Jewish voters are concerned he was the strongest possible candidate the Republicans could nominate for Governor in 1954. His misfortune was to run against Averill Harriman. Harriman, well known for his services to Roosevelt and Truman in various administrative and diplomatic posts, conducted a New Deal-Fair Deal campaign. He attacked the Dewey record in New York, and even blasted the Eisenhower administration in Washington. As a consequence Harriman garnered a higher percentage vote in 1954 in Jewish assembly districts in New York than Stevenson had won in 1952. In many districts Ives ran behind the Dewey vote for President in 1948 as well as behind Eisenhower in 1952. In some districts his percentage vote was actually as low as the Dewey vote for President in 1944, when Jewish support for Roosevelt was almost monolithic.

Another liberal candidate on the Republican ticket was expected to make even greater inroads on the Jewish Democratic vote than Senator Ives. He was Representative Jacob Javits, candidate for the office of Attorney General. Javits, like Case, was known in Congress as a New Deal Republican. He and Case consistently turned in the worst party voting records during their stay in the House of Representatives. Moreover, Javits is a Jew and a militant Zionist. There were still other factors in his favor. He was active in civic reform efforts in New York City, always popular among most Jews. He spoke out openly for a more liberal immigration policy, increased aid to Israel, support for the UN, and even advocated changing the UN into a world federal government. He always received firm support from Jewish voters in his own neighborhood in Washington Heights when he ran for Congress, running as much as 40 per cent ahead of Eisenhower in the most Jewish election districts in the 15th Congressional District in 1952. As a congressional candidate, Javits had the support of New York's Liberal Party. In 1954 the Liberal Party opposed him and supported his opponent, Franklin D. Roosevelt, Jr. Roosevelt's campaign was disappointing to many of his friends, but his name was still magic to large numbers of Jewish voters. When he made his first campaign visit to the boardwalk at Coney Island older Jewish men and women crowded around to cheer him, and one lady rushed up to kiss his hand. Javits, in an amazing upset, survived the Democratic tide and was elected Attorney General, but he did not run as well as had been expected in Jewish districts. In his own assembly district Javits ran far ahead of Ives, but in other Jewish areas his vote was surprisingly low. In Brooklyn's 2nd, 15th, and 16th A.D.s the former congressman received merely 19.8, 10.2, and 21.7 per cent of the total vote for Attorney General. In the 7th A.D. in the East Bronx, Javits received 23.1 per cent of the vote. Nearby, in the lower Concourse region, in the 2nd A.D., he only won 17.5 per cent, actually running behind the Eisenhower percentage vote for 1952. Harriman and Roosevelt showed that liberal Democrats can still swamp liberal Republicans in Jewish districts, even when one of the Republicans is a Jew.

Liberal Republicans have had a difficult time in Jewish districts since 1952, but not nearly so difficult as for representatives of the conservative wing of the Party. A clear-cut contest in Illinois between Senator Paul Douglas and neo-isolationist Republican Joseph T. Meek for Douglas' Senate seat resulted in a smashing victory for Douglas in all Jewish districts in Chicago. Meek is a prototype of midwestern conservatism. He has expressed favorable opinions on Senator McCarthy and on the Bricker amendment to limit Presidential power in foreign affairs. During the campaign he looked unfavorably on foreign economic aid, the New Deal, and the United Nations. Douglas, a scholarly ex-Professor of Economics at the University of Chicago, was first elected to the Senate in 1948, when he ran ahead of Harry Truman in all of Chicago's Jewish neighborhoods. His ability and thoroughness as a Senator had won him general praise. As a liberal Democrat he was frequently mentioned as a Presidential possibility, but chronic illness prevented him from taking such suggestions seriously.

The extent of Douglas' victory in Jewish districts in 1954 was larger than his most optimistic backers had hoped for. He ran well ahead of 1950 Democratic Senatorial candidate, Scott Lucas. The Douglas vote cannot be accounted for only by the weakness of Meek as a candidate. Meek was simply a smaller, less famous version of Lucas' opponent in 1950, Senator Everett M. Dirksen, another pronounced conservative and nationalist. In the five most Jewish precincts in Albany Park's Ward 40—over 90 per cent Jewish—Douglas received 91.1 per cent of the vote. In other Jewish neighborhoods the sweep was repeated. In the old ghetto on Chicago's West Side there are twenty-two precincts in Ward 24 which are more than 90 per cent Jewish. There, Douglas won 92.7 per cent of the votes cast for Senator. Up on the North Side near Lake Michigan, in heavily Jewish precinct 31 of Ward 49, the ex-college professor captured 80 per cent of the vote, twice the proportion received in any neighboring Gentile precinct. In Ward 4, precinct 35—about 75 per cent Jewish— he received 77.5 per cent of the votes recorded. In the Jewish precincts in Wards 46 and 48 the ex-Marine won similar triumphs. In the seven middle-class precincts of West Garfield Park, the Senator ran ten per cent ahead of the Lucas vote in 1950 and seventeen per cent ahead of the vote for Stevenson in 1952. In fact, he ran far ahead of the percentage Stevenson vote in all Jewish districts.

Since 1952, Jews have apparently sustained their Democratic loyalties. Three factors have worked against the Republicans more than any others. First, the right wing of the G.O.P. has continued to be vocal and influential despite the election of Eisenhower. Senator McCarthy was often deferred to by the White House during the first two years of the Eisenhower administration. The President refused to speak out openly against the Senator and appointed pro-McCarthy men to such key posts as Federal Communications Commissioner and Security Officer in the State Department. Even with the demise of McCarthy, the Knowland, Bricker, Jenner, Bridges, and Dirksen wing of the party is a formidable group which must be reckoned with in shaping Republican policies.

A second factor hurting Republican chances with Jewish voters has been the administration policy toward Israel and the Arab states. Zionist leaders have publicly decried the Administration's unwillingness to take a moral position between the two sides in the Middle East. Zionists cannot understand why the State Department ships arms to feudal Arab leaders and holds back on military aid for the Israeli democracy. When individual Republican leaders such as Ives and Javits have denounced the shipping of arms to Arab countries, they have been rebuffed by Washington. More than twenty Zionist rallies were held throughout the country in October, 1954, a few weeks before the general election, protesting Administration policy towards Israel. Representatives of sixteen large Jewish organizations called on Secretary of State Dulles to urge the United States to extend the same kind of military and political agreements to Israel which were given to Arab states. At a mass nonpartisan meeting in New York, Republican leaders were given a rough going over by nearly all the speakers. A favorite target was Vice-President Richard Nixon, who was ridiculed for a charge he was alleged to have made that Zionists were misrepresenting Administration policy in the Middle East.

Still a third factor militating against a Jewish switch to the Republican Party has been the emergence of dozens of new Democratic leaders with a liberal bent. Since 1948 a large number of latter-day New Dealers have scored successes in American politics. In fact, the Democratic Party has been rejuvenated in nearly all of the states with large Jewish populations within the last few years. The liberal factions of the Party have become more influential in recent years from California to New York. In New York City itself, Jews are probably more active in the New York County (Manhattan) organization than at any time since the early days of the Republic. Many of them represent insurgent reform forces tolerated in Tammany under the regime of Carmine DeSapio. For the first time in several decades the Democrats of New York nominated liberals to run for the Senate, for Mayor, and for Governor in successive elections in 1950, 1953, and 1954. The New Deal faction is more powerful now than at any time since the death of Franklin Roosevelt. Herbert Lehman is in the Senate, Robert Wagner is Mayor, and Averill Harriman lives in the Governor's mansion.

While no fundamental rehabilitation of the Democratic Party has occurred in Massachusetts, the Democrats did nominate a non-Irish liberal for the United States Senate in 1954. Foster Furculo was the first Italian to run state-wide as a Democrat, and almost was elected. On the same ticket with Furculo in four Boston wards and in the towns of Brookline and Newton was a young Jewish lawyer, liberal Jackson Holtz, candidate for the House of Representatives from the 10th Congressional District. No Jewish Democrat had been elected to Congress from Massachusetts since Leopold Morse went to Washington in the nineteenth century, but Holtz almost won an amazing upset victory in what was considered a safe Republican district. Endicott Peabody, another Fair Dealer, did win a surprise election to a seat on the Governor's Council. Never in the memory of some of Boston's oldest electors have such names as Furculo, Holtz, and Peabody all appeared on the Democratic ticket in one year.

A number of New Deal Governors have been elected in

other states in recent years. In Pennsylvania, where the Democratic Party has undergone a thorough overhauling, George Leader ran exceptionally well in Jewish districts in Philadelphia and Pittsburgh in 1954. G. Mennen Williams in Michigan and Robert Meyner in New Jersey are vigorous young products of the New Deal philosophy. Abraham Ribicoff, the first Jew to be elected Governor of any state in almost 20 years, won in Connecticut in 1954. Ribicoff, the first American Governor of Russian-Jewish descent, and Congressman Thomas Dodd, who even ran ahead of the Governor in Jewish districts in Hartford, are other liberal-internationalist Democrats whose predilections were shaped in the atmosphere of the New Deal. It was Ribicoff who told a radio-television audience during the campaign that "only in the Democratic Party could a boy named Abe Ribicoff be nominated for Governor." While even Ribicoff would admit the inexactness of his claim when applied to the rest of the country, the fact is that all of the eight Jews in the House of Representatives and the two Hebrews in the United States Senate are liberals and Democrats. The newest Jewish Senator is Richard L. Neuberger, a progressive in the tradition of George Norris, who surprised the experts by his election to the Senate from Oregon where the Democratic Party was supposed to be in a coma.

These are the factors which make it difficult for liberal Republicans to successfully woo the Jewish vote: the Republican right wing, the administration's policy in the Middle East, and emergent liberal leadership in the Democratic Party. Of course, there is one great asset on the Republican side, Dwight Eisenhower. Should the President, in spite of his heart attack, again be the Republican standard bearer in 1956, many Jewish voters might turn to him as the architect of peace. From his dramatic visit to Korea soon after his election to the big power talks at Geneva, Eisenhower's one political passion has been peace. If the President does not stand for re-election, American Jewry would look with considerable favor on the candidacy of Chief Justice Earl Warren, who has demonstrated his devotion to Negro rights, civil liberties, and welfare government. Vice-President Nixon, on the other hand, has never been popular in the American Jewish community. He would have to work hard to overcome the reputation he has established for opportunism and what the liberal press has called "white-collar McCarthyism." Any Republican candidate will still have to make his peace with the more belligerent and conservative faction within the Party. The three leading Democratic contenders, Stevenson, Harriman, and Kefauver are all warmly received by most Jewish groups. Each has criticized the refusal of the administration to meet the 1956 Israeli request for arms purchases in this country. Each is a representative of the New Deal wing of the Democratic Party. Provided the Democrats continue to espouse the policies of Roosevelt in foreign and domestic matters, the Jewish attachment to the Democratic Party should continue regardless of who the Republican candidate is. Whether Jewish voters will remain as solidly Democratic as they have in the past or whether they will begin to divide their vote more sharply along class lines will depend, of course, upon the candidates, the issues, and the voters' perception of them.

CHAPTER VIII

Independent Beginnings:
The Socialist Tradition

THOSE PECULIAR JEWS

As EARLY as 1898, social workers in the South End of Boston commented on the unpredictability of the Jewish vote.[1] "The Jews [of Boston]," wrote Frederick A. Bushee in 1903, "are not wedded to any party or faction, and the handling of their vote is a strain on the sagacity of even an Irish politician."[2] The previous year, when the Jews were probably the largest single ethnic group in Boston's West End, one observer wrote:

> The Jew is a thorn in the flesh of the Irish politician. . . . At first the Jews so imperfectly understood the political game that they formed educational clubs to influence their people without regard to the party affiliations of prospective citizens. Such conduct is incomprehensible to Irish politicians.[3]

Another West End settlement worker noted, "They [the Jews] are very difficult material for the politician. They are individualists, quarreling constantly among themselves. . . ."[4]

In New York the story was the same. The Jews would

1. Robert A. Woods, editor, *The City Wilderness, op. cit.,* pp. 134-135.
2. Frederick A. Bushee, *Ethnic Factors in the Population of Boston* (New York: Macmillan Co., 1903) , p. 132.
3. Robert A. Woods, editor, *Americans in Process* (Boston: Houghton Mifflin & Co., 1903) , p. 64.
4. *Ibid.,* p. 160.

not settle down and be Republicans or Democrats like ordinary people. One worker observed in 1907 that the Jews of the East Side were mugwumps, often splitting their tickets, or voting for minor party candidates. He wrote that they "form the great portion of the uncontrollable and unapproachable vote of the ghetto. . . ."[5] Three years before, an editorialist for the *Nation*, studying the returns from the heavily Jewish 8th Assembly District, wrote:

> This is the district with the largest foreign population, and its population is very largely Jewish. It has such well known ghetto streets as Hester, Delancy, Eldridge, and Allen. Yet politically it is one of the most uncertain sections; the majority of the winning candidate is always small. It voted for Bryan in 1900; for Roosevelt in 1904; for Coler in 1902; for Higgens this year. Its representative at Albany is alternatively a Republican and a Democrat. The Tenth District, which also shows signs of independence, is strongly Jewish.[6]

The 8th, the 10th, and 16th, all heavily Jewish for the first decade of the century, were known for their independence. First ticket-splitting, then surging Socialist strength characterized those neighborhoods.

In Chicago the picture was not different. The Jews, constituting a majority of the 9th Ward, were responsible for small majorities given to Bryan in 1900 and Roosevelt in 1904.[7] Roosevelt won there by more than 900 votes despite the fact that the Democratic candidate for Mayor, Carter Harrison, carried the 9th by 1679 votes in 1903. Left-wing third-party candidates always fared well in Chicago's Jewish neighborhoods. In 1899, the famous Altgeld, running as an Independent for Mayor, received 750 votes in Ward 9. Three years later in the heavily Jewish 17th Senatorial District Clarence Darrow received 6,000 votes as an independent candidate.

---

5. Emanuel Hertz, in *The Immigrant Jew in America*, edited by Edmund J. James (New York: B. F. Buch & Co., 1907), p. 261.
6. *The Nation*, December 1, 1904.
7. Elija N. Labine, in *The Immigrant Jew in America*, op. cit., p. 277.

THE MAJOR PARTIES DRESS ALIKE

The peculiarity of the Jews lay in their inability to cast their lot with either of the major parties. Neither major party showed any consistent attachment to the interests of the Jews. At the national level those interests were the very same which have drawn the Jews to the Democratic Party these last three decades—internationalism and welfare government. Bryan for the Democrats and Roosevelt for the Republicans appeared to be interested in expanding federal power for the welfare of all citizens, but the issues which were hot one moment sputtered and fizzled the next. On the subject of internationalism neither party had much to say. Leaders in both parties were agreed that the United States ought to keep out of European affairs, and that Europe ought to keep out of the Western Hemisphere.

In local affairs the Jews were interested in reform. With few exceptions they did not benefit from the corruption of local Democratic machines in New York, Boston, and Chicago. Too often they found the Republican organization in alliance with the Democrats. They welcomed independent, nonpartisan organizations and candidates which condemned Democrats and Republicans alike. In New York City they bulked large among the reform forces that organized the Citizens Union in 1897. They were important in the defeat of Tammany in the Mayoralty contest in 1901. In the first Seth Low campaign "congregations of pious Jews saying their Shabbas Eve prayers folded their shawls and supplanted their prayers by feverish political meetings."[8] Not so feverish were the prominent German Jews of New York City, but they were no less anti-Tammany than their Russian brethren. Jacob Shiff, Oscar Straus, Isaac Seligman, and Henry Morgenthau all joined the various movements for independent reform government which appeared in the city from time to time.

---

8. Simkovitch, *op. cit.*, p. 66.

SOCIALIST STRONGHOLDS

There was one political party, an international party already known to many Jews before they came to America, which militantly advanced programs of interest to a great many Hebrews—the Socialist Party. It called for international brotherhood, urged the welfare state, and denounced Tammany and Republican venality with puritanical fervor while preaching the gospel of reform.

The reform plank in its platform may have been its best vote-getter. Socialists won more supporters by denouncing local corruption than by casting visions of the millenium. As sound politicians, many Socialist leaders saw that local corruption worried and local reform interested the religious and serious Jews of the ghetto. As one Socialist wrote later,

> The immigrant masses saw their homes polluted by gamblers . . . they saw themselves robbed by cheap little leaders who grafted on peddlers and extorted money from tenants, and they began to realize that the task of those who wanted a better world was not to dream of revolution in Russia, but to fight Tammany Hall in New York.[9]

So the Socialists talked as much of honest elections and new bath houses as they did of government ownership of the railroads and international justice.

The Socialist strongholds were the Jewish ghettos. As one settlement worker recalled, "the real university of the East Side was Marx's *Capital*. Read like the Bible with faith, like the Bible it formed the taste and moulded the life of its readers. Socialism as an economic theory is one thing," she continued, "as an education it is another. It is what we are excited about that educates us. What the East Side was excited about was Socialism."[10] While young men and women elsewhere contrasted the virtues of McKinley and Bryan, an unusual number of the immigrant Jews discussed anarchism,

---

9. Harry Rogoff, *An East Side Epic: The Life and Work of Meyer London* (New York: The Vanguard Press, 1930), p. 15.

10. Simkovitch, *op. cit.*, p. 63.

socialism, and other radical creeds, sometimes choosing from among them as if they were the only alternatives available.

TRADE UNIONS

To the immigrant Jews of New York, the two most important sources of political opinion were the trade unions and the Yiddish newspapers. The leadership of both was predominantly Socialist. The United Hebrew Trades, the first co-ordinating Jewish union, was started in 1888 by leaders of the Socialist Labor Party. The UHT was successful in organizing thirty-two unions under Socialist auspices. The labor movement brought forth a number of labor newspapers. In 1890 the *Abeiter Zeitung* became the first Yiddish Socialist newspaper in America. It was followed by the Socialist monthly, *Die Zukunft,* and then by the *Abendblatt,* which was controlled by the radical Socialist Daniel De Leon. Finally, the influential Socialist *Jewish Daily Forward* was founded in 1897 under the editorship of Abraham Cahan. By 1918, when the *Forward* lost its mailing privileges, its circulation had reached 200,000, far more than that of any other Yiddish paper. As late as 1938 the results of a survey of the Jewish community in Stamford, Connecticut revealed that more than one out of every ten Jewish families there still subscribed to the *Forward.*[11] The *Arbeiter Ring* or Workmen's Circle was another product of the Jewish Socialist labor movement. It was organized in 1892 by a half dozen Jewish Socialists and anarchists as a fraternal association. Reorganized in 1900, it eventually had many millions of dollars in property and tens of thousands of members in the United States. Its leadership has been primarily Socialist throughout its history.

TWO SOCIALIST TITANS

The two Socialist titans of New York's lower East Side were Morris Hillquit and Meyer London. Each possessed

---

11. Samuel Koenig, "Sociometric Structure of an American Jewish Community," in *Jews in a Gentile World,* edited by Isaque Graeber and Steward H. Britt, (New York: Macmillan, 1942) , pp. 234-235.

overpowering personalities. Each was an intellectual, a born leader, and a tireless worker in the cause of Socialism. Both of them were Jews, though neither of them were orthodox. Louis Waldman, who subsequently was elected and re-elected to the New York State Assembly as a Socialist, told of the first time he heard Hillquit speak in 1911. Wrote Waldman,

> He commanded the breathless attention of the audience with his first few words. His thought was clear, logical and every sentence which he spoke was uttered with purity of diction which transformed everything he said into literature. . . . It is thirty-two years since the night of that meeting and I still recall vividly every word he spoke, remembering it as though it were yesterday.
>
> Never in my life had I been held and fascinated as I was by this speaker. . . . The audience stood and cheered when he concluded, and since I had not caught his name when he was introduced I turned to my neighbor and asked who the orator might be.
>
> Incredulously, the man replied: "Do you mean to tell me you've never heard Morris Hillquit before?"[12]

Hillquit, who was five times a candidate for the House of Representatives from predominantly Jewish districts, was a household word in Jewish homes. He always polled a very heavy vote, although he was beaten four times and counted out a fifth. He ran first from the 9th Congressional District, an area covering only one square mile which held a population of 200,000, most of whom were Russian-Jewish immigrants. The old 9th was a dependency of Tammany Hall. Purchasing of votes was common. Floaters and repeaters were often used, and the local Republican organization worked in cynical association with the Tammany machine. That year William Randolph Hearst's Independence League gave its endorsement to Tammany's Henry M. Goldfogle, to assure Hillquit's defeat. So frightened were the Hearst forces and

---

12. Louis Waldman, *Labor Lawyer* (New York: E. P. Dutton & Co., 1934), pp. 35-36.

the Democrats by Hillquit's showing that they enlisted the support of the Republican organization in 1908 to beat Hillquit again.

A few years later the 9th Congressional District was incorporated into the 12th Congressional District, which by then was preponderantly Jewish, but which had very large Irish, Italian, and German minorities. This time Hillquit, who could always count on about 40 per cent of the total vote in Jewish congressional districts, was counted out by a Democratic-Republican alliance in favor of the regular Republican, Isaac Siegel. The regular organizations used every trick to beat him. They always ran an orthodox Jew against him, and challenged Hillquit's lack of religious orthodoxy. They always settled on just one candidate—usually a Democrat, once a Republican—to support in fusion. But in 1910 they had to resort to a phony count to beat the tireless Socialist.

His last great effort was in the Mayoralty campaign of 1917. He campaigned as a Socialist against the Independent reform candidate, John F. Hylan, and the popular Democrat, John P. Mitchell. Yet, Hillquit won a plurality in the three most Jewish assembly districts in New York County. In those districts Hillquit and Hylan, the minor party candidates, received more than five times the vote cast for Mitchell, the regular Democrat.

It will forever be impossible to know the true strength of the Socialists in Jewish districts during the first two decades of this century. Many immigrant Jews could not vote, and year after year many were robbed of their true vote by Tammany's venal methods. Sluggers, floaters, and repeaters were used to beat the Socialists; votes were purchased in the rooming houses, saloons, and red light districts; ballots were mutilated, and ballot boxes stolen. An honest count was impossible.

Tammany stopped Hillquit, but it could not always overwhelm that other East Side giant, Meyer London. London, who came to this country from the Ukraine at the age of fifteen, was an East Side hero, another grand figure in the history of American socialism. He was a perennial candidate for office, running first for the State Assembly (from the 4th A.D.) in 1896 and 1898 as a Socialist Labor candidate and again in 1904 under the banner of the new Socialist Party. All of the weapons in the arsenal of the regular organizations could not prevent the election of London to the House of Representatives from the 12th Congressional District in 1910. To help him win, the growing cloakmakers' and furriers' unions which London had befriended in earlier days organized cadres of workers. He was backed by the *Jewish Daily Forward,* extending its influence constantly. His workers came from the Socialist Workmen's Circle, ever increasing its role as a center of Yiddish cultural and social activities. More than one hundred union locals "imbued with Socialist principles" and "led by Socialist leaders" with a membership of over 200,000 championed Meyer London.[13]

London was beaten in 1914 by Hillquit's old nemesis, Henry Goldfogle, but the Socialist came back strong in 1916. Then London was opposed by an active Zionist, Tammany's Judge Sanders, who "tried to make his chief issue London's lack of Jewishness.[14] But Sanders failed. Friendly unions organized special campaign committees, provided London with men who had served on picket lines to watch the polls and pass out literature. And "London received the overwhelming vote of the Jewish citizens of . . . the district."[15]

Two years later London was beaten by a few hundred votes. He lost to Goldfogle who was sponsored by a fantastic assortment of Socialist haters. The Republicans joined Tammany and the Zionists joined the Communists, who had just begun to pull away from the Socialist Party.[16] And they all worked together to beat the indefatigable London. Non-

---

13. Rogoff, *op. cit.,* pp. 48, 56.

14. *Ibid.,* pp. 119-120.

15. *Ibid.*

16. In 1919 the Socialist Party split into three separate groups: the Communist Party with an estimated membership of 50,000; the Communist Labor Party, estimated membership 25,000; and the Socialist Party, 25,000.

Socialist Jews flayed him for having attended a session of Congress on Yom Kippur, the Day of Atonement. Former President Theodore Roosevelt denounced London as a weakling. Yet, all of the fury of the combined opposition managed to unseat London for two years only. He was back again in 1920 and was elected against a fusion of all parties including the Republican and newly formed Communist Party.

During this period Jewish assembly districts elected and re-elected in the face of combined major-party opposition a number of Socialists to the state legislature. The decade which was split by the outbreak of the great war in France was the period of peak strength for Jewish Socialists. Wilson, with his New Freedom, had raised to the level of respectability many of the issues which Socialists had been talking about for years. The great war itself provided Socialists with an opportunity to stir the interest of Jews in international brotherhood.

SOCIALIST RESIDUE

Jewish socialist strength subsided from the peak years leading up to and during World War I, although Norman Thomas ran well in Jewish districts in his quest for the Presidency as late as 1932. The residue of earlier Jewish socialism has settled in a variety of political movements in recent decades. Many lifelong Socialists hailed Roosevelt's New Deal and left militant socialism forever. When Abraham Cahan returned from Europe shortly after New Deal messages started to flow from the White House, he told a large gathering of Socialists in New York's Madison Square Garden to give up their theories and back Roosevelt's specific policies. Sooner or later a majority of the Jewish Socialists followed Cahan's advice. The Socialist vote toppled in Jewish districts between 1932 and 1936. Some Socialist deposit went into the formation of new parties of the left in New York. Not happy with supporting Roosevelt as a straight Democrat, the top Jewish labor leaders in 1936 started

The American Labor Party. While returning from a CIO meeting in Washington, Max Zaritsky urged David Dubinsky and Sidney Hillman to form a new labor party. "It can nominate Roosevelt, too," he said, "and workers who don't want to vote Democratic can vote for him this way." In 1936 the American Labor Party polled 274,924 votes for Roosevelt, immediately becoming a force in New York politics. When Communists succeeded in infiltrating the ALP in 1944, Dubinsky, Alex Rose, and others withdrew, and formed the Liberal Party, which has ever since replaced the ALP as the important third party in New York.

While the least militant socialists became Liberals or Democrats, a small minority, dissatisfied with the respectable leadership of Norman Thomas, drifted into the Communist movement. Though small in numbers, they played a major role in the leadership of the Communist Party in the 1930's and 1940's. A Department of Justice study in 1947 showed that 56.5 per cent of the militant Communist Party members listed in its files were born either in Russia or in adjacent countries.

The early Socialist tradition among Russian Jews has influenced the contemporary political behavior of their children and grandchildren in a variety of ways, but the main impact has been to promote independence at the polls.

CHAPTER IX

Splitting Tickets

INDEPENDENT VOTERS

THOUGH THE Jews have turned in very substantial pluralities
for Democratic Presidential candidates, they do not consider
themselves to be overwhelmingly Democratic. They prefer,
rather, to think of themselves as independents. Whenever
members of ethno religious groups have been asked to desig-
nate their party affiliations in sample surveys, the percentage
of self-designated independents is always much higher among
Jews than in any other group. This was true in national
surveys in 1940, 1944, and 1948.[1] It was true in a sample of
college graduates in 1948.[2] It was true in a sample of voters
in Pittsfield, Massachusetts in 1952,[3] and it was true for the
sample surveyed in Ward 14 in Boston. Only in 1944 did a
majority of Jews, 54 per cent, in a national sample report
that they considered themselves Democrats.

The reputation of the Jews for electoral independence
(inconstancy to either major party) and their own self-
concept as independents is largely deserved. They have not

1. Robert T. Bower, *op. cit.*, see Table XII.
2. Ernest Haveman and Patricia Salter West, *op. cit.*, p. 194. Fifty-eight
per cent of the Jewish college graduates called themselves independent
compared to forty-one per cent of the Catholics and thirty-two per cent
of the Protestants.
3. Philip K. Hastings, "The Independent Voter in 1952: A Study of
Pittsfield, Massachusetts," *American Political Science Review*, Vol. XLVII,
No. 3 (Sept. 1953), p. 805. It ought to be pointed out that there were only
eleven Jews in the Pittsfield sample. Six called themselves independent. In
the Ward 14 sample, thirty per cent of the Jews called themselves independent as compared to twenty-two per cent of the Gentiles, not as large
a gap as is usually found.

given their favor to all Democrats, it seems, but only to those who in the Jewish view were liberals and internationalists. The Jews have not been as kind to Democratic candidates for lesser office as they were to Roosevelt, Truman, and Stevenson.

There are two basic ways in which the Jews have shown independence from the Democrats in recent decades. One way has been by splitting tickets, voting for some candidates from one party and some from another. The other way has been by voting for minor party candidates. Faced with anomalies in our party system, the Jews have tended to split their tickets and to vote for minor party candidates more than other voters have.

The nature of the American political party system has forced inconstancy on the Jews. Our national parties are alliances of state and local organizations which are some-times highly incompatible. Democratic candidates for state office in Virginia have been conservatives while Democratic candidates for state office in New York have often been liberals. Democratic candidates for the Senate from Massa-chusetts have been isolationists while those from Connecticut have been internationalists. When liberal and international-ist Republicans are offered as alternatives to conservative and isolationist Democratic candidates, many Jews jump the Democratic ship. When candidates from both major parties are conservative and isolationist, some Jews give third party candidates their vote.

WHY THE JEWS SPLIT TICKETS

The phenomenon of ticket splitting is a source of in-terest to diverse observers of the political scene. It holds the attention of academicians—witness the attention they give to ticket splitting as an analytic tool; it surprises the politicians —observe their chagrin at failing to hold their precincts all along the line; and it pleases the leaders of civic betterment organizations and the editorial writers for our independent dailies—note their acceptance of ticket splitting as a mark of intelligence and rationality. In this regard, there has been no group more interesting, surprising, and pleasing than the Jews. Since 1924 they have been, relatively speaking, prodigious ticket splitters.

The reasons for Jewish ticket splitting are not hard to find, and indeed, have already been stated. It has been shown how the Jewish group interests in internationalism and liberalism have been primarily responsible for the whopping pluralities given by the Jews to Democratic Presidential candidates since 1932. To a lesser extent the same interests have shaped Jewish voting preferences for non-Presidential offices as well. Most Jews would no more have voted for an isolationist candidate for Governor or Senator in 1944 just because he was the Democratic candidate than they would have voted for Thomas Dewey just because his program suited their economic interests.

It is true that the interest of American Jewry in liberal government and in internationalism generally transcends party lines, but the importance of the liberalism and the internationalism issues only partially explains the Jewish penchant for ticket splitting since 1924. It must be remembered that candidates for Governor and for Congress run on local as well as national issues, and a large number of Jews have not always found the Democratic position on local issues as compatible with their own views as the Democratic position on national and international questions.

"Reform" and anti-regular Democratic histories have been inherited by Jewish communities in almost every large city. Wherever substantial reform movements have sprung up, regardless of whether the city was controlled by Republicans or Democrats, Jews have tended to support the reform group. In most cases the local Democratic organization was under fire. But in Cincinnati, where civic reform has been more successful and lasted longer than anywhere else, Jewish leaders helped to topple a Republican political machine from power. Individual Jews such as State's Attorney General Gilbert Bettman sided with the organization, but the vast majority of his coreligionists joined Murray Seasongood and Julian Pollack in supporting the City Charter movement to usher in a system of proportional representation and the city manager plan. Much of the leadership in the district and ward organizations as well as a substantial part of the funds for the Charter Committee came from Cincinnati Jewry. The anti-Tammany tradition in New York and the anti-Irish feeling in Boston have been discussed previously. Jacob Javits is fond of telling how he became a Republican in reaction to Tammany venality. His father, a building superintendent in the lower East Side, was often given the job of passing out dollar bills to pay off the faithful. Largely because of the strength of reform sentiment among Jews in New York and Boston, the Jewish Republican attachment persisted in the early 1920's with respect to candidates for state and local office long after the Jews had abandoned Republican Presidential candidates. The Jews did not break their local Republican ties as quickly as they dropped G.O.P. contestants for the White House. In New York, Roy Peel reported that just as many Jews belonged to Republican clubs as belonged to Democratic clubs as late as 1935,[4] although the Jews of New York gave Roosevelt 90 per cent majorities in 1936. In Boston the pattern was similar. In 1928 only 39 per cent of the voters in Ward 14 cast ballots for Hoover, but 75.3 per cent of the primary voters there participated in the Republican primary. In 1932 only 29 per cent of the votes in Ward 14 went to Hoover, but 46.4 per cent of the primary voters that year (66.5 per cent the year before) participated in the Republican primary. The Jewish involvement in the Republican organization in Boston continued even after the election of Roosevelt. As late as 1934 no Jew even contested to represent Ward 14 on the Democratic State Committee, while all the candidates for the Republican State Committee from Ward 14 were Jewish as they had been for a number of years.

---

4. Roy Peel, *The Political Clubs of New York* (G. P. Putnam's Sons, 1935) , p. 259.

All of these factors—vestigial Republican affiliations, the anti-Tammany and anti-Irish traditions, the reform tradition, and the liberalism and internationalism of the Jews—often caused Jewish dissatisfaction with Democrats on the state and local level in Detroit,[5] Philadelphia,[6] Chicago, Boston, and New York, and such dissatisfaction was often manifest in split ballots.

ANOMALIES IN BOSTON

The Jews of Boston appear to have been inveterate ticket splitters these past three decades, and indeed, a great many of them have probably never voted a straight ticket. Boston Jews are neither more idiosyncratic nor more rational than Hebrews elsewhere. The fact is that on some issues of importance to the Jews the Republican Party in Boston and Massachusetts appears to have been in agreement with Democratic Presidents. On the other hand, the Democratic leadership in the Commonwealth has often been out of sympathy with the Roosevelt-Truman-Stevenson view in matters of foreign policy and civil liberties.

A look at specific cases will show how such anomalies result in Jewish ticket splitting. An index of approximate net ticket splitting is provided in *Table 11*. The method used to compute approximate split-ticket voting (finding the percentage difference in the vote for two candidates on the

---

5. Jewish precincts in Detroit were still giving the Republican Gubernatorial candidate eighty per cent of their vote as late as 1934. Donald Hecock, *Detroit Voters and Recent Elections* (Detroit: The Detroit Bureau of Governmental Research, Inc., 1938), p. 14.

As E. H. Litchfield showed, a high percentage of Russian-born (Jewish) voters in Detroit persisted in claiming Republican affiliation long after the Jews had become a heavily Democratic voting group in Presidential elections. E. H. Litchfield, *Voting Behavior in a Metropolitan Area* (Ann Arbor: University of Michigan Press, 1941) p. 43.

6. In Philadelphia the two Italian areas which showed the highest deviation between party vote (Democratic) and party affiliation (Republican) in Presidential elections "contain Jewish voters who usually exhibit some independence" according to Hugo V. Maiale, *The Italian Vote in Philadelphia Between* 1928 *and* 1946, Ph.D. Thesis, University of Pennsylvania, 1950, p. 64.

same ticket) does not yield an index of the actual extent of split-ticket voting in these four wards because voters crossing party lines in opposite directions are canceled out in the total figures. Given the ethnic homogeneity of these particular wards[7] and the consistency of the higher percentage difference in Ward 14, it is certainly possible to conclude that Jewish voters in Boston have split their tickets much more frequently than others. Closer inspection of individual elections mirrors the play of factors which cause this type of independence.

TABLE 11

**APPROXIMATE NET TICKET SPLITTING IN FOUR BOSTON WARDS,
FOR PRESIDENT AND SENATOR**

Year	% Difference in Vote for Democratic Candidates for President and for Senator*			
	Ward 3	Ward 5	Ward 14	Ward 15
1928	+ 6.3	+ .5	+21.2	+ 2.3
1932	No Senatorial contest			
1936	− 5.3	−10.4	−32.5	− .9
1940	+ 8.1	0.0	−34.9	+17.0
1944	−21.8	−22.2	−50.9	−19.0
1948	− 5.3	− 7.4	−15.3	− 8.3
1952	+ 2.3	+ 2.6	−11.4	+12.1
Average % Difference	8.2	8.9	25.9	9.9

7. See the methodological notes at the end of the book for further information on the four Boston wards. Throughout this period the Italian concentration in Ward 3, the Irish concentration in Ward 15, and the Jewish concentration in Ward 14 has never been less than sixty-five per cent or more than eighty-five per cent. Ward 5 has been predominantly Yankee since 1924, although it now holds a large transient population in rooming houses and hotels and is increasingly Irish.

* A plus sign signifies that the Democratic candidate for Senator ran ahead of the Democratic candidate for President. A minus sign means the Senatorial candidate ran behind.

The Democratic candidates for the Senate in 1936, 1940, and 1944 were James M. Curley, David I. Walsh, and John Cocoran. In Irish Ward 15, Curley and Walsh ran ahead of Roosevelt, but Curley received only 51 per cent of the Ward 14 vote in 1936 while F.D.R. won 83.5 per cent. And in 1940 Walsh received merely 54.4 per cent of the votes cast there compared to 89.3 per cent for Roosevelt. In 1944 Cocoran, less well known than either Curley or Walsh, won only 41 per cent of the Senatorial vote in Ward 14 although Roosevelt, running at the head of the ticket, received a record percentage of 91.9.

The Republican opponents of Curley, Walsh, and Cocoran were in many ways more friendly to Jewish interests, at least as the Jews saw them, than were the Democrats. Henry Parkman, Jr., Henry Cabot Lodge, Jr., and Leverett Saltonstall were generally considered internationalists in foreign affairs and liberals in domestic matters. They were all brahmans of respected lineage. Each was respectable enough to be considered completely above anti-Semitism.

In 1936 Lodge ran against Curley. There were many things in Curley's favor as far as Boston Jewry was concerned. He had just completed his first term as Governor, during which he had sweated out of his legislature a liberalized workmen's compensation law, a pro-labor anti-injunction statute, and a forty-eight hour work week. He had won Jewish favor as early as 1911, when he made a fight in Congress against restrictive immigration legislation and for abrogation of the Russian trade treaty which discriminated against American Jews. During the campaign Curley told rally after rally how many Jews he had appointed to public office, and recalled that Lodge's grandfather had led the fight in the Senate against the confirmation of Louis D. Brandeis' appointment to the Supreme Court. Yet, Curley ran 32.5 per cent behind Roosevelt in Ward 14. Lodge, a candidate for the Senate for the first time, and relatively unknown, received about as many Jewish votes in Boston as James Curley. Curley was the victim of sharp tension between Jew and

Irishman in Boston in 1936. The core of his support came from Charlestown, South Boston, and other Boston Irish strongholds where anti-Semitism flourished. Although Curley attacked Father Coughlin, he could not deny that he had once been a friend of the Michigan anti-Semite, and he could not easily disavow local Coughlinite support. Lodge attacked the Governor for his notorious scrapes with the law, and won Jewish votes for his progressive stand on the issues of the campaign.

In 1940 Henry Parkman, Jr. ran 34.9 per cent ahead of Wendell Willkie in Ward 14. Probably four out of ten Boston Jews who voted for Roosevelt also voted for Parkman. A long tradition of philanthropy was associated with the Parkman name. Henry's cousin, George, had left everything he had, about five million dollars, to the city of Boston for parks and playgrounds. Henry, Sr., who ran very well in Ward 14 in the Mayoralty election of 1933, had also given most of his money to charities. Parkman, an internationalist, made it clear that he accepted the basic reforms wrought by the New Deal. Parkman's opponent, David Walsh, was well supported by Jews in 1934 as an out-and-out progressive, but by 1940 he was an isolationist candidate.[8] Thousands of Jewish voters saw no inconsistency in crossing party lines to vote for Roosevelt and Parkman.

In 1944 probably more than five out of every ten Jewish voters in Ward 14 cast ballots for Roosevelt and Saltonstall, a Democrat and a Republican. Saltonstall, whose ancestors arrived on the Arabella in 1630, made a record in the State Legislature which won him a reputation for impeccable honesty and for friendliness to labor and minority groups.

---

8. Jewish dislike of Walsh because of his isolationism was very great. It lasted until the end of the late Senator's career. In 1946, for example, only 3,525 Democratic primary voters in Ward 14 cast ballots for Walsh even though he was the only candidate on the ballot. On the same day, 5,492 Democrats voted for John McCormack in Ward 14 for renomination as candidate for Congress though McCormack was unopposed too. McCormack was an internationalist.

Not only was his record liberal on domestic issues, but he was a strong internationalist (as were Yankees Parkman and Lodge) at the very time when the fortunes of the British Empire and Western Europe were bound up with those of Europe's enslaved Jewry. When Saltonstall allowed himself to be quoted as calling F.D.R. "Our Great President," there remained little doubt in the minds of Jewish voters where he stood on the issues of our time. His adversary, John Cocoran, made an inept campaign. He ran badly everywhere, but nowhere so poorly as in Ward 14, where his association with regular Democracy, his Irishness, his failure to emerge as a liberal and internationalist, all were counted against him.

Jewish voters did not desert Democratic gubernatorial candidates as readily as they left the candidates for the Senate. The major reason for this is plain. International or foreign policy issues did not figure prominently in the gubernatorial campaigns. Still, many Jews crossed party lines to vote for Republican candidates for Governor in 1936, 1940, and 1944. In 1936 and 1944 Charles F. Hurley and Maurice Tobin, the Democratic gubernatorial candidates ran well in Ward 14 compared to other candidates for state office, but vestigial Republican affiliations there were strong enough to help their Republican opponents, John W. Haighs and Horace T. Cahill, run well ahead of Landon and Dewey. Tobin, considered to have been a liberal and an internationalist, received nearly 70 per cent of the votes cast in Ward 14, but he could not come close to matching the tremendous vote for F.D.R. In 1940 Saltonstall was the Republican candidate for Governor. He had already completed one term, and as already stated, he was unusually popular with the Jews of Boston. While Saltonstall's Democratic opponent, Paul A. Dever, ran ahead of Roosevelt in Irish and Italian wards, he ran 37.9 per cent behind F.D.R. in Ward 14. The percentage differences in the vote for Democratic candidates for President and Governor for four Boston wards as shown below in *Table 12* indicate that Jews split many more ballots than non-Jews in presidential election years.[9]

TABLE 12

APPROXIMATE NET TICKET SPLITTING IN FOUR BOSTON WARDS,
FOR PRESIDENT AND GOVERNOR

Year	% Difference in Vote for Democratic Candidates for President and for Governor*			
	Ward 3	Ward 5	Ward 14	Ward 15
1928	— 2.3	— 1.5	— 7.3	— 6.1
1932	+ 6.0	+11.1	+ 7.4	— .2
1936	— 4.3	— 6.5	—16.4	+ 9.3
1940	0.0	— 6.7	—37.9	+ 6.0
1944	— 2.4	— 5.3	—22.9	+ 1.8
1948	+ 7.6	+ 4.7	+ 5.5	+ 6.7
1952	0.0	— .8	— .4	+12.2
Average % Difference	3.2	5.2	15.7	5.3

It is apparent that the enthusiastic response of Boston Jewry to Democratic Presidential candidates did not extend to Democratic senatorial and gubernatorial running mates, with a few exceptions. It is also true that Republicanism in the Commonwealth of Massachusetts is not without appeal for the Jewish population of Boston. Such are the anomalies within our federal system which prompt the Jews of Boston to split their tickets so often.

CONSISTENCY IN NEW YORK

A look at approximate split-ticket voting in New York City in Presidential years since 1924 sheds considerable light

9. There will be a further discussion of gubernatorial candidates later in the section on split-ticket voting for state offices.

* A plus sign signifies that the Democratic candidate for Governor ran ahead of the Democratic candidate for President. A minus sign means the gubernatorial candidate ran behind.

on the nature of Jewish "independence." The votes for the Democratic candidates for President from 1924 through 1952 were compared with the votes recorded for the senatorial or gubernatorial candidates on the same ticket in the Bronx Second A.D. (Jewish) and in Richmond County (Gentile). The percentage difference was considered to be an approximation of split-ticket voting. Although the average percentage difference was higher in the Bronx Second A.D. than in Richmond, only in one year, 1924, is the difference in the Bronx exceptionally large. Then John Davis, the Democratic Presidential candidate, ran 46 per cent behind Al Smith, the Democratic gubernatorial candidate in the Second A.D. Davis' Wall Street background was against him in Jewish areas with their tradition of Socialist activity. Moreover, the national platforms of the major parties were almost indistinguishable. Smith, on the other hand, though an Irish Catholic, was close to the Jews of New York. New York Jewry, not hopelessly outnumbered by the Irish as they were in Boston, were more secure and less hostile to the sons of Erin. Moreover, ethnic tension between the two groups was relatively low because of general prosperity at home and the absence of Hitlerism abroad. Still more in Smith's favor was the fact that he was a liberal. His ideas for the administration of the state of New York were precursors of the New Deal.

Thousands of Jews supported this East Side hero, a son of immigrant parents, but were unwilling to vote for Davis. They split their ballots for Coolidge, who had singled the Jews out for favorable public utterances, or for LaFollette, whose views on public policy were most compatible with those of Smith. LaFollette, who had the backing of the Socialist Party, actually ran ahead of both Coolidge and Smith in the most Jewish assembly districts in the Bronx, Brooklyn, and Manhattan. A split ballot for LaFollette and Smith was for many Jews an index of constancy to principles more than a measure of inconstancy to parties.

The figures on approximate split-ticket voting for New

York show that Jews do not cross party lines when candidates for Presidential and lesser offices represent the same political program. Though Smith and Davis appeared to be incompatible to many Jews in 1924, they found Roosevelt and Robert F. Wagner, the Democratic Senatorial candidate, most congenial in 1944. While John Cocoran, candidate for the Senate from Massachusetts, ran 50 per cent behind Roosevelt in Ward 14, Wagner and Roosevelt received almost exactly the same proportion of votes on the tickets of all three parties which sponsored them in the Bronx Second A.D., as may be seen in *Table 13* below. Few Jews split tickets in the Bronx in 1944, because Wagner and Roosevelt campaigned on the same issues. Indeed, Wagner warmly championed all of the causes associated with the name of Roosevelt. Wagner was an outstanding liberal and internationalist. His Republican opponent, Thomas Curran, was a conservative Republican County leader in Manhattan. In Boston many Jews split tickets. The Republican Senatorial candidate was a liberal and internationalist, and the Democratic candidate for the Senate was an unknown quantity.

TABLE 13

JEWISH TICKET SPLITTING IN THE BRONX, 1944

Party	% F.D.R.	Total Vote	% Wagner	Total Vote
Democratic	45	23,299	45	22,991
Liberal	20.3	10,691	20.7	10,545
A. L. P.	19.3	9,982	19.4	9,939
Total	84.6	43,972	85.1	43,475

SPLITTING TICKETS IN BOSTON IN 1952

There was considerable split-ticket voting among both Jews and Gentiles in Ward 14 in 1952, as the results of the sample survey conducted there show. Of the 135 Jews who said they voted for Stevenson, at least 66.7 per cent crossed party lines to vote for George Fingold, the Jewish Republican candidate for Attorney General. More than 24 per cent of the Stevenson voters in the sample voted for Henry Cabot Lodge, Jr., Republican Senatorial candidate, and 23.7 per cent cast ballots for Christian A. Herter, the successful Republican aspirant for Governor. One out of every three Jews in the sample who voted for Eisenhower voted for John Kennedy, Democratic Senatorial candidate, and almost the same proportion voted for Governor Paul Dever in his bid for re-election.

Gentile voters in the sample (mostly Irish Catholics) who voted for Eisenhower crossed party lines to vote for Kennedy almost as frequently as Jews split tickets to vote for Fingold. Forty-three per cent of the Christians who voted for General Eisenhower for President also cast ballots for the boyish Irish Democrat for Senator. In addition, 38.9 per cent of the Gentile Eisenhower electors voted for Democrat Francis Kelly against Fingold for Attorney General, although at least 12 per cent of these did not cross party lines to vote for Kennedy.

Almost as many Gentiles, it appears, split tickets in Ward 14 in 1952 as Jews. At least 50 per cent of the Jews and 45 per cent of the Gentiles did not vote a straight ticket. In the case of the Jews it was the Stevenson voters who crossed over to mark ballots for Herter, Lodge, Fingold, and Mintz (Jewish Republican candidate for Auditor) ; with the Gentiles it was primarily the Irish Catholic voters for Eisenhower who switched to choose Dever, Kennedy, Kelly, and Buckley (Irish Catholic candidate for Auditor.)

The causes of Christian ticket splitting were many. The terrific attraction of Eisenhower to normally Democratic voters was a major factor. Another was that Stevenson, a Unitarian, was the only non-Irish Catholic on the Democratic ticket running for state or national office. Of the Republican candidates for state office, two, Lodge and Herter, were descendents of Mayflower Anglo-Protestantism and two, Fingold and Mintz, were the sons of Russian Jewish immigrants.

Turn Irish Catholic motivations upside down and the

causes of Jewish ticket splitting in Ward 14 in 1952 are made apparent. Republicans Fingold and Mintz were Jewish, although it must be added that Kelly did badly among all groups because of charges imputing dishonesty to him and because of his rowdy campaign. As Eisenhower was attractive to many Irish Catholic voters, so Stevenson was appealing to the Jews. Herter, formerly an internationalist Congressman from a district comprising Jewish Ward 12, represented to many Jews the possibility of non-Irish reform government in the Commonwealth. Lodge ran ahead of both Eisenhower and Herter in Ward 14 because of his very pronounced internationalism.[10] In Brookline's most Jewish precinct the pattern was repeated. Mintz and Fingold ran ahead of the ticket. Lodge ran ahead of Herter and Herter ahead of Eisenhower. More than three out of five Jewish Stevenson voters in Brookline switched parties to vote for Fingold. As many as one out of every four may have split tickets to vote for Lodge. The same factors which cause ticket splitting among Jews in middle-class Ward 14 promote that phenomenon among Jews in Brookline.

SPLIT-TICKET VOTING FOR STATE OFFICE

The percentage difference between the Democratic vote cast for Governor and Lieutenant Governor in fourteen elections from 1926 through 1952 were compared for the four Boston wards in order to approximate the amount of ticket splitting in contests for state office. It is generally expected that candidates for these two offices on the same ticket will run very close. These candidates are rarely divided along ideological lines or by important issues of any kind. It might be supposed, then, that any substantial difference in strength between these two could be accounted for by

10. Widely circulated attacks were made on Kennedy and his father, Joseph P. Kennedy, former Ambassador to the United Kingdom, to the effect that either or both were anti-Semitic. Some Jews were in doubt as to Kennedy's internationalism. One Democratic politician in the Ward surreptitiously did what he could to hurt Kennedy.

personality differences, how well known the candidates are, personal organizational strength, and the conduct of their campaigns (finances, speaking ability, etc.) .

However, analysis of state elections reveals that the voters of Ward 14 do not always perceive the candidates for Governor and Lieutenant Governor on the same ticket to represent similar political points of view. Factors such as speechmaking ability, personal following, familiarity of name, and position on the ballot would be likely to affect all voters equally. But there have been few elections since 1926 when the Jews of Ward 14 did not split more ballots than the voters in the three control wards. In fact, the average percentage difference in the vote cast for the Democratic candidates for the two highest state offices from 1924 through 1952 is twice as great in Ward 14 as in Yankee Ward 5, almost three times as great as in Irish Ward 15, and more than four times as large as in Italian Ward 3.

LIBERALS OR CONSERVATIVES?
IT MAKES A DIFFERENCE

The attraction or repulsion of Jews for candidates for state office, even for the office of Lieutenant Governor, depends in good measure upon whether the Jews perceive the contestants as liberals or conservatives. An examination of the five elections in which the Democratic candidate for Lieutenant Governor ran either ten per cent or more behind or ahead of the head of his ticket supports that proposition.

In 1932, Governor Joseph B. Ely, a candidate for re-election, ran 20.2 per cent ahead of his running mate, John E. Swift, in Ward 14, where Ely received the highest vote ever given by Boston Jews to a Democratic gubernatorial candidate.[11] Jewish voters thought of Ely as a liberal, broad-minded Protestant who, in his first term as Governor, led the fight for a huge public works program, unemployment relief,

---

11. The fact that Ely won so high a vote is even more remarkable when it is considered that Socialist candidate, Alfred Baker Lewis, received 9.2% of the ballots cast in Ward 14.

and the regulation of holding companies and railroads. Ely, in short, like Al Smith in New York whom he greatly admired, had given the citizens of the Bay State a Roosevelt-type New Deal for two years before the election of F.D.R. as President.[12]

By way of contrast, Ely's running mate, John Swift, was a slightly known Irish politician who had no record as a liberal. His Republican opponent, Gasper G. Bacon, had as President of the Massachusetts State Senate gained a reputation as a progressive Republican and, like Ely, was thought to be something of an intellectual. Aside from these factors the Jews of Ward 14 had a special reason to look with favor on Bacon's candidacy. As President of the Senate in 1930 he had written the lead article in an anniversary edition of the *Jewish Advocate,* Boston's single large Jewish (English language) newspaper entitled "Jewish influences on Massachusetts and America." While less than two out of every ten Jews in Ward 14 voted for Ely's adversary, William Youngman, more than half of them cast ballots for Bacon, indicating a large-scale splitting of tickets.

Two other years in which Jewish ticket splitting for state offices apparently was high were 1940 and 1942. Leverett Saltonstall, already known for his first term as Governor, for his internationalism, and for his admiration of Franklin Roosevelt, was the Republican candidate for Governor in both contests. Saltonstall's opponent, Paul A. Dever, could win only 51.4 per cent of the votes. However, Dever's running mate for Lieutenant Governor, Owen A. Gallagher, did considerably better against the undistinguished incumbent Lieutenant Governor, Horace T. Cahill. In 1942 again the popularity of the long-faced Saltonstall was too much for his Democratic opponent, Roger Putnam, who lost by 3,000 votes in the Ward. And so Cahill ran 14.3 per cent behind Saltonstall.

---

12. Ely later followed Al Smith into the Liberty League and attacked Roosevelt in 1936. Had the Jews of Ward 14 been able to foresee Roosevelt's accomplishments and the subsequent attack by Ely, it is doubtful that the latter would have fared so well in 1932.

In 1946 the Democratic candidate for Governor, Maurice J. Tobin, ran 13.9 per cent behind Dever, who was candidate for Lieutenant Governor in Ward 14. Irish Catholic and Jewish ticket splitting tendencies in this one instance seem almost identical. In this one case the explanation of Jewish ticket splitting does not revolve primarily around the perception of the candidates by the Jews as liberals or conservatives. Tobin was known to be a liberal and was friendly with many Jews, as already reported.

Tobin's opponent, Robert Bradford, was a strong candidate. He had won a wide reputation as a crusading District Attorney who had gone far in purging Middlesex County of criminal elements. Dever's Republican foe, on the other hand, was Arthur W. Coolidge, who did nothing to dispel the feeling that his thinking on public questions was similar to that of the former President whose surname he bore. But the answer to Jewish ticket splitting in 1946 lies also in the superb organizational job which the Dever forces did in Ward 14. Paul Dever had run three times before for state office, and each time increased the percentage vote cast for him in that area. The two primary sources of Dever strength in Ward 14 lay in his reputation as a reform-minded Attorney General and his cultivation of Jewish politicians.

In 1952, Dever, in his unsuccessful quest for re-election as Governor, ran 12.3 per cent ahead of Jeff Sullivan, Democratic candidate for Lieutenant Governor, in Ward 14 despite the fact that Dever's opponent, Herter, was known to be an internationalist Congressman. Sullivan impressed Jews as an orthodox Irish politician, while the Republican candidate for Lieutenant Governor, Sumner Whittier, vigorously campaigned for "clean" and "reform" government. Whittier ran well everywhere, but he was especially strong in Ward 14 where he received 1,000 votes more than General Eisenhower. One woman who switched from Stevenson, Dever, and Kennedy explained her vote by saying that Whittier looked "so like my brother" whose picture she carried in her wallet. But most Jewish ticket splitters in 1952 were not whim voters. Many crossed over because they were in conflict about the issues of the gubernatorial campaign. They wanted a continuation of the social services and building program of Dever (liberalism as they saw it), and they also wanted reform and honesty in state government. A vote for Dever was a vote for the continuation of the New Deal and Fair Deal in the Bay State; a vote for Whittier was a vote against kickbacks, corruption, and Irish Catholic government.

Thus, the splitting of tickets by Jewish voters, even in elections for state office, is often a function of the Jewish perception of candidates as liberals or conservatives, internationalists or isolationists.[13] It is also a function of Jewish attraction to national Democrats on the national issues and repulsion from local Democrats on some issues. The Jewish attraction to reform candidates, no matter which party they come from, is a major factor in the production of ticket splitting. When city elections are held in different years than elections for national and state office, ticket splitting cannot occur, but there is often an abrupt change in major party loyalties in Jewish districts. Recent mayoralty elections in Chicago illustrate the point. In 1947 the Democratic candidate for Mayor, businessman Martin Kennelly, campaigned on a reform program. In nearly every Jewish precinct in Chicago Kennelly was rewarded with the highest vote ever given to a Democratic candidate for Mayor. Seven years later ex-Democrat reformer Robert Merriam ran for Mayor on the Republican ticket, and converted many Jewish votes in middle-class and upper-middle-class neighborhoods. Whereas Kennelly received 75.1 per cent of the vote in the ten most Jewish precincts of Ward 48 in 1947, Merriam captured 53.8 per cent in 1955. In the nine most Jewish precincts of

13. The same conclusion applies to Gentile voters in Ward 14 too. While Roosevelt ran far ahead of Dever and Walsh in 1940 in Jewish areas, he ran well behind them in Irish areas. Had Saltonstall and Parkman, both liberal pro-British internationalists been on the Democratic ticket, the Irish electors in Ward 15 would have certainly split many more tickets than the Jews of Ward 14.

Ward 46 the Democratic vote for Mayor fell from 67.8 per cent to 45.6 per cent.

Beyond the Jewish penchant for reform candidates, ticket splitting is often a measure of consistency in the Jewish approach to the political issues of our time. In the sample of Jewish voters in Roanoke, Virginia (discussed in Chapter VII) 70 per cent of the Stevenson voters expressed disapproval of conservative Democratic Senator Harry F. Byrd while 70 per cent of the Eisenhower voters said they approved of Byrd. That is why almost half of the Stevenson voters in the sample voted for an anti-Byrd liberal Republican for Governor in 1953. For voters who are issue-oriented rather than party-oriented, there is a great deal more logic in splitting tickets or switching parties than in changing ideas. Oscar Straus summed it up in 1908 when he was asked to explain why he had switched from the Democratic Party to the Republicans. The Secretary of Commerce and Labor answered that he did not switch from one side of the fence to the other, but that the fence itself had moved.

CHAPTER X

Minor Parties

MANY STUDENTS of politics have noticed Jewish third party tendencies in recent decades. Wrote one political observer in 1935, the Jews in New York "far outnumber all other groups in attendance at meetings in minor party clubs and headquarters."[1] In Detroit, Edward Litchfield noticed that the Russians (Jews) always gave minor party candidates for Governor twice the support given them by other groups in the motor city during the 1930's.[2] The Jewish support everywhere for LaFollette in 1924 and Wallace in 1948 have often been commented on.

SOCIALISTS IN NEW DRESS

The story of Jewish socialist leanings during the first two decades of the century has already been told in Chapter VIII. For many reasons—including the stigma attached to opposition to the war, the general prosperity of the twenties, class mobility in America—the strength of the Socialist and other Marxist parties ebbed until Socialist candidates no longer represented a serious threat to the major parties at the polls. But socialist thinking and feeling among American Jews did not die out. In some cases Jews were satisfied in the 1930's and 1940's that candidates for the major parties had adopted the socialist ideals of the welfare state and international brotherhood. In other cases new parties of the

---

1. Roy Peel, *op. cit.*, p. 259.
2. Edward H. Litchfield, "A Case Study of Negro Political Behavior in Detroit," *Public Opinion Quarterly*, Vol. 5 (June, 1941), p. 273.

left arose from socialist remains with less offensive names and dress to capture the loyalties of old Jewish socialists. And wherever and whenever the Socialist parties still presented candidates, they always fared better in Jewish neighborhoods than anywhere else.

MINOR PARTY VOTING IN PRESIDENTIAL
ELECTIONS: IN NEW YORK

The pressures on Socialists to change their name were great in the State of New York. During the war, duly elected Socialist Assemblymen were actually refused their seats by a conservative state legislature. Socialists were painted in the press and by major party politicians as foreign saboteurs, men with long hair, women with short hair, destroyers of home, church, and property. When Robert LaFollette ran for President as a Progressive, a name with respectable associations, he won pluralities in Jewish assembly districts and precincts in New York. Finally, in 1936, the left-wing American Labor Party was formed, and since that time the voters of New York have always had an opportunity to vote for a Democratic candidate for President and a substantially socialist program at the same time without having to mark a Socialist ballot. The Jews of New York have seized this opportunity to approve of Roosevelt, Truman, and Stevenson and at the same time express dissatisfaction with the Democratic Party. Since 1936 the minor party vote in the Bronx Second A.D. has never been less than 15 per cent of the total vote for President. In 1944 it was almost 40 per cent (all for Franklin Roosevelt). Richmond voters, as might have been expected, eschewed the opportunity to vote for a Democratic Presidential candidate on a radical platform. If they felt dissatisfaction with the Democratic Party or its candidates, as many have since 1940, they voted Republican, the only right-wing choice available to them. A comparison of the extent of minor party voting in Richmond and the Bronx Second A.D. appears below.

TABLE 14

MINOR PARTY VOTING IN THE BRONX AND RICHMOND,
PRESIDENTIAL ELECTIONS

Year	Bronx Second A.D.	Richmond
1924	24.9	9.9
1928	2.1	.5
1932	10.1	3.5
1936	14.7	3.3
1940	16.7	4.1
1944	39.6	4.9
1948	34.3	5.1
1952	22.3	2.4

When Jewish voters thought Democratic candidates were overly conservative they turned in heavy votes for non-Communist or Socialist Progressives, Robert LaFollette and Henry Wallace. Whereas these two averaged 27.3 per cent of the votes cast in the Bronx Second A.D., they received an average of merely 6.8 per cent in Richmond County.

IN BOSTON

The Jews of Boston were not as fortunate as their co-religionists in New York. No American Labor Party or Liberal Party emerged as an outgrowth of the early socialist movement. Only in four elections from 1928 through 1952 did minor party candidates receive more than one per cent of the total vote cast in any of the four Boston Wards under study. In three of these contests the voters of Ward 14 turned in the highest percentage minor party vote. In each of these elections, 1928, 1932, and 1948, the minor parties were left wing parties—in 1928 and 1932 the Socialist, Socialist Labor, and Workers (Communist) Parties, in 1948 Henry Wallace's Progressive Party. While an average of about nine out of every hundred Jewish votes cast in Boston in those three elections went to left-wing candidates, an average of less than one out of every hundred Gentile votes went to these same men.

In 1936, however, the percentage minor party vote was largest in Ward 15, not Ward 14, as may be seen in *Table 15*. While the left-wing minor party candidates again fared better in Ward 14 than elsewhere, the Irish voters of Ward 15 turned in a large third party vote for Lemke and O'Brien, the candidates of the Union Party. For many Irish voters the Democratic candidate in 1936 was too liberal, and they were happy to have a chance to vote for the right-wing candidates endorsed by Gerald L. K. Smith and Father Coughlin. In poorer Irish Wards than 15, such as Wards 2 and 6, Lemke actually received almost as many votes as Landon. If a right-wing minor party candidate had been available to the Irish in 1940, 1944, and 1952, when they were somewhat unhappy (as the Jews were pleased) with the Democratic candidate, perhaps they would have turned in high minor party votes in those years as well as in 1936. On the other hand, had the Jews of Boston an opportunity to vote for Roosevelt, Truman, and Stevenson on the Massachusetts equivalent of the American Labor and Liberal Parties of New York, the minor party turnout in Ward 14 would have been consistently higher than it actually was.

TABLE 15

MINOR PARTY VOTING FOR PRESIDENT IN FOUR BOSTON WARDS

Year		3	5	14	15
				Wards	
1928		.9%	.1%	3.6%	.02%
1932		2.8	3.1	9.6	.9
1936	left wing	1.0	1.1	1.3	.5
	right wing	3.4	3.7	2.2	12.6
1940		1.0	.04	.1	.03
1944		*all under one per cent*			
1948		2.8	4.2	12.3	1.5
1952		.4	.4	1.0	.2

MINOR PARTY VOTING IN MAYORALTY CONTESTS
IN NEW YORK

A review of minor party voting in state and city-wide contests in New York City shows that Jewish inconstancy to major parties is even heightened in non-Presidential contests. The minor party vote in the Bronx Second A.D. and in the control area, Richmond County, were compared for Mayoralty contests over a twenty-five-year period beginning with the 1925 election. Then, Norman Thomas, the Socialist candidate, received 5.2 per cent of the votes recorded in the Second A.D., but only 0.6 per cent of the votes cast in Richmond. Four years later Mr. Thomas increased his Second A.D. vote to 16 per cent, almost as high as recorded for Fiorello LaGuardia, who was then running for Mayor for the first time on the Republican ticket. In 1932 the great Socialist, Morris Hillquit, won 22.4 per cent of the Second A.D. vote and only 4.1 per cent of the Richmond vote. That year the combined vote of Socialist, Socialist Labor, and Communist mayoralty candidates was double that of the Republican nominee in the Second A.D.

In 1933 LaGuardia won a minor party nomination for the first time. Running on the City Fusion ticket, he was able to win thousands of votes in the Second A.D. that had been cast for Socialists just the year before. To a preponderance of Jewish voters "The Little Flower" combined the New Deal philosophy and the program of Roosevelt with the civic reformism of Robert Moses. The Jews of New York thenceforth always turned in large pluralities for LaGuardia —but under a minor party label and not the Republican banner.

The turbulent, pint-sized Italian was a natural success among Jews. By 1933 he was well known to many of them. Although it was not often advertised, his mother was one-quarter Jewish. In his first few years in politics he made many Jewish contacts. In the garment strikes of 1912 and 1913, "He drew up briefs and argued cases, representing his penniless clients without expectation of remuneration. He worked on committees and even served in the picket line."[3]

LaGuardia made his first run for Congress as a Republican in 1914 in an East Side Tammany bailiwick which had a considerable Jewish population. He made an anti-Tammany fight against the popular Michael Farley without the support of regular Republicans and lost by only 1700 votes where a Democrat had never failed to win by less than 16,000 votes before. His biographers agree that it was the votes of enthusiastic Hebrews which nearly elected LaGuardia to the House of Representatives, "Storming up and down hallways, he exchanged sparkling repartee in Yiddish with fat Jewish matrons and bearded skull-capped Rabbis," who took LaGuardia to their hearts.[4]

One year later, as Deputy Attorney General for the State of New York, the irrepressible LaGuardia publicly denounced as hypocritical a recent order of the Czar of Russia emancipating Jewish subjects so that they might serve in the army. His remarks on the Czar were "reprinted in the Yiddish press," and they "made a deep impression on the New York ghetto. He was favorably spoken of in synagogues as the champion of an oppressed people."[5] In 1916 LaGuardia again ran for Congress and this time, the recipient of increased Jewish support, retired Farley from congressional affairs.

Only in 1918 did LaGuardia have trouble with Jewish voters. His difficulties did not come from the Democrats, since Charles F. Murphy had made a deal with the Republicans in exchange for Republican support elsewhere. But a pacifist-socialist, Scott Nearing, vigorously campaigned against Major LaGuardia, and won enough Jewish support to scare both Republicans and Democrats despite the fact

3. Lowell M. Limpus and Burr Leyson, *This Man LaGuardia* (New York: E. P. Dutton & Co., Inc., 1938), p. 28. Much of the material on LaGuardia presented here comes from this lively biography.
4. *Ibid.*, p. 31.
5. *Ibid.*, p. 36.

that he was under indictment for violation of the Espionage Act at the very time.

In Congress, LaGuardia continued to champion the Jews. He introduced a resolution warning Russia and Poland to expect no friendship or aid from the United States unless the governments of those countries stopped abusing their Jewish populations. In 1919 LaGuardia was persuaded to leave Congress to run for Alderman in a heavily Jewish district from which he was easily elected. Failing to win the mayoralty nomination in 1920, he campaigned again for election to the House of Representatives from the 20th Congressional District, then composed primarily of Jews and Italians, against the Jewish Tammany leader, Henry Frank, and the Socialist, William Karlin. LaGuardia stole the Socialist's thunder by calling for a minimum wage law, old age pensions, child labor restrictions, national maternity legislation, abolition of labor injunctions, the direct primary, an eight hour work day, equality of opportunity for women, freedom of speech for radicals, the initiative and the referendum, and unrestricted immigration. He was also for modification of the Volstead Act to permit the sale of light wines and beer, opposed censorship of films, and was in favor of international action to outlaw war. His program was radical, his approach inspirational. As he explained it to Jewish audiences, then slightly sour on Warren Harding, he was a Republican in name only:

> I am a Republican, but I am not running on the Republican platform. I stand for the Republicaness of Abraham Lincoln; and let me tell you now that the average Republican leader East of the Mississippi doesn't know any more about Abraham Lincoln than Henry Ford does about the Talmud.[6]

Despite ridiculous charges of anti-Semitism leveled against him by Tammany (he answered them in Yiddish), LaGuardia beat Frank and Karlin, and went back to Con-

---

6. *Ibid.*, p. 136.

gress where he worked tirelessly for the end of prohibition, against the Ku Klux Klan, for a child labor amendment to the Constitution, for pacific measures in international relations, and against immigration restrictions. With this kind of liberalism, LaGuardia kept winning in the 20th Congressional District as long as it was predominantly Jewish. In 1932, in an increasingly Italian District, LaGuardia was finally beaten by an Italian Democrat, presumably riding on Roosevelt's coat tails.

The Jews who moved from the 20th Congressional District to the Bronx did not leave their LaGuardia sentiment behind them. In the 1933 mayoralty campaign already referred to, LaGuardia drew his greatest strength from New York's Jewish population. In the Bronx "Flynn leaders could scarcely believe their eyes when they received the reports of their first midsummer canvass. The precinct workers reported an almost unbelievable sentiment for LaGuardia."[7] It has been reported that Flynn first decided to run Judge McKee as an Independent against Tammany's O'Brien when he realized the extent of reform sentiment among Bronx Jews.

The thousands of Jewish votes which LaGuardia received in Jewish areas in the Bronx in the election were duplicated in Jewish neighborhoods everywhere in the city, and "most political experts agreed that it was the shifting of this vote (from the Democratic and Socialist Parties) which turned the tide toward LaGuardia."[8] Although the diminutive Italian received twice as many votes under the City Fusion label as he did Republican votes in the Second A.D., exactly the reverse was true in Gentile Richmond County.

The minor party vote for LaGuardia and for all minor party mayoralty candidates has been consistently higher in the Second A.D. than in Richmond, as may be seen by a glance at *Table 16*.

---

7. *Ibid.*, p. 362.
8. *Ibid.*, pp. 368-369.

TABLE 16

MINOR PARTY VOTING FOR MAYOR IN THE BRONX AND RICHMOND

Year	Bronx Second A.D.	Richmond
1925	5.6%	0.5%
1929	16.6	8.2
1932	38.8	16.7
1933	59.9	50.2
1937	43.7	18.1
1941	42.8	9.1
1945	57.2	23.2
1949	44.9	8.2
1950	55.1	62.7
1953	44.4	7.1

LaGuardia continued to do things that pleased the Jews. He was even more outspoken than Roosevelt in denouncing Hitler for his outrageous treatment of German Jewry, publically calling the Fuehrer a "brown-shirted fanatic" in 1937. Just one year after Roosevelt had received 82.4 per cent of the votes cast for President in the Bronx Second A.D., the Republican candidate for Mayor, LaGuardia, won 65.2 per cent of the vote, two-thirds of these under minor party banners.

Again, in 1941, LaGuardia received almost twice as many minor party votes in the Second A.D. as he did Republican votes. Mr. Flynn's candidate could muster only 33.1 per cent of the vote cast there just one year after Roosevelt had won 78.2 per cent of the Presidential vote.

In 1945 the minor party vote for Mayor in the Second A.D. rose to 57.2 per cent of all ballots cast, two and one-half times the percentage minor party vote recorded in Richmond. LaGuardia's disciple and ex-President of the City Council, the blue-blooded and silk-stockinged Newbold Morris, received one out of every four votes cast in the Second

A.D. on the newly formed and never-to-be-revived No Deal ticket. Only 13.1 per cent of the minor party vote went to the nominee of the Liberal Party, Jonah J. Goldstein, who was nominated by the Republicans in an effort to remove some of the bad feeling left by anti-Semitic aspects of the 1944 Presidential campaign. Goldstein was a popular, cigar-chewing Tammany Democrat who, as Judge in the Court of General Sessions in Manhattan, had been active in Jewish and other communal affairs. In politics he was more noted for his organizational orthodoxy than his ability to formulate and discuss the issues. Despite the fact that he was a Jew, the only Jew in the race, his campaign failed to interest the Jews. He could not easily denounce Tammany, his principal source of benefaction; nor could he blast the Republicans under whose flag he so dully campaigned. Unable to say the things that the generality of Jewish voters want mayoralty candidates to say, he could not win their substantial support. Knowing the strength of Jewish third party tendencies, Governor Dewey and others expected to consolidate the Jewish vote in the Liberal Party in 1945. Failing to nominate a clear-cut, pro-New Deal, anti-Tammany liberal, they lost badly in the attempt.

On the other hand, the Irish Catholic William O'Dwyer, having received the nomination of the Democratic Party, and the special endorsement of liberals such as Herbert Lehman and Eleanor Roosevelt, also won nomination from the American Labor Party. As the ALP candidate, O'Dwyer received more Jewish votes than Goldstein won under the Liberal Party banner. And Newbold Morris, the LaGuardia-backed anti-Tammany candidate, won more Jewish votes on the No Deal ticket than Goldstein received as a Republican and Liberal combined.

In 1949 Morris was nominated for Mayor by the Liberal Party. LaGuardia sentiment among Bronx Jews was hard to dissipate despite the identification of Mayor O'Dwyer, Democratic candidate for re-election, with the New Deal elements of the Democratic Party in New York. Morris won better than three out of every ten Jewish votes in the Second A.D., five times the percentage of minor party votes as were counted in Richmond.

In fact, there has only been one year in which the percentage minor party vote in Richmond was higher than in the Second A.D. Only in 1950, when the Richmond Democratic leadership backed Vincent Impelliteri against the regular Democratic nominee, Justice Ferdinand Pecora, did the Gentile electors from Staten Island turn in a higher minor party vote than the Jews from the Bronx. The contest within Richmond was factional. The leadership there dramatized Impelliteri as an independent who had not been given fair recognition for his past services as President of the City Council and as Acting Mayor. The campaign also had slight ideological overtones. Although there was no real issue between the Impelliteri forces and the regular Flynn and Tammany Democrats, Pecora did receive the support of New Deal elements in the party while the conservative leaders backed the genial Acting Mayor. In the Second A.D. half of the minor party votes cast went to the ALP and Liberal candidates, Ross and Pecora. In Richmond they received a meagre 4.5 per cent of the minor party vote; Impelliteri won all the rest.

So great is the Jewish propensity for voting for minor party candidates for Mayor that it would have been impossible for the Democrats to carry the Second A.D. or other Jewish districts without minor party help. There is no doubt that many sons and daughters of East Side radicalism carried the political predispositions of their fathers with them to the Concourse even though they left their depressed living standards behind. Indeed, the percentage of minor party enrolled voters actually was twice as high in the Second A.D. in 1952 (8.4 per cent enrolled in the Liberal and American Labor Parties) than it was in 1924 (4.2 per cent enrolled in the Socialist Party). In Richmond, minor party enrollment has gone down from 1.6 per cent to 0.6 per cent during these same twenty-eight years.

MINOR PARTY VOTING FOR
GOVERNOR IN NEW YORK

As shown in *Table 17*, there have been twelve gubernatorial elections in New York since 1924. During that time
the percentage minor party vote for Governor has always
been higher in the Second A.D. and all Jewish neighborhoods than in Richmond and other Gentile areas.

TABLE 17

**MINOR PARTY VOTING FOR GOVERNOR
IN THE BRONX AND RICHMOND**

Year	Bronx Second A.D.	Richmond
1924	5.3%	1.0%
1926	6.5	1.3
1928	2.4	0.5
1930	11.5	3.4
1932	7.4	3.8
1934	10.9	5.2
1936	15.9	4.7
1940	25.1	5.1
1942	35.9	5.8
1946	39.1	4.3
1950	30.0	4.3
1954	19.1	2.9

In the first eight of these contests the Democratic candidates were considered liberals. Al Smith ran twice, Franklin
Roosevelt twice, and Herbert Lehman four times. Since, in
their own time, they each spoke for the New Deal or liberal
wing of the Democratic Party, they were all received with
favor by Jewish voters. To many Jewish voters these liberals
stole the thunder of the Socialists. Thus, the combined Communist and Socialist vote in the Second A.D. from 1924
through 1934 was never higher than 11.5 per cent, which it
reached in 1930.

When the American Labor Party was organized in 1936 and gave its nomination to the Democratic nominee, Herbert Lehman, Jews were afforded the chance to vote for a liberal for Governor who could be elected and at the same time support a more radical platform than the one offered by the Democrats. Herbert Lehman, like Roosevelt and LaGuardia, was (and still is) a political hero to American Jewry. He is perhaps the most prominent Jew ever elected to public office in the United States. The son of German-Jewish immigrants successful in the banking field, the young Lehman early decided upon a career of public service. In 1930 he was elected Lieutenant Governor of New York State, running ahead of gubernatorial candidate Franklin Roosevelt. He was subsequently elected Governor in four successive campaigns. Even when he was defeated in his first bid for a Senate seat in 1946, a Republican year, he ran 400,000 votes ahead of his ticket. He was, of course, especially popular among Jews. Lehman received a high ALP vote in 1936 and increased that vote in 1938 by 12 per cent. The combination of Lehman and the ALP was effective in taking votes away from Socialist candidate Norman Thomas, who received less than one per cent of the vote in the Second A.D., formerly a Thomas stronghold. The campaign between Lehman and racket-busting Thomas E. Dewey was tense. As in 1936, when Coughlinites attacked Lehman, overt anti-Semitism was a feature of the campaign. Because of this and related international issues, Republican Fiorello LaGuardia finally endorsed Lehman after having promised to be Dewey's campaign manager. When the results were in they showed that Dewey carried Christian upstate New York by 619,000 votes while Lehman won in New York City by 683,000 votes. And for every two Jews who cast ballots for the Governor as a Democrat, one checked his name alongside the ALP symbol.

In 1942 the Democrats nominated a conservative to run for Governor for the first time in eight elections. John J. Bennett, an Irish-Catholic supporter of Franco, failed to receive American Labor Party support, and large numbers of Jews balloted for minor party candidates. Educator Dean Alfange received 31.1 per cent of the votes cast for Governor in the Second A.D. (less than five per cent in Richmond) on the ALP ticket, and even the Socialist and Communist candidates profited in Jewish neighborhoods by the failure of the Democrats to nominate a liberal, receiving more votes than they had since 1934.

In 1946 the Democrats nominated ex-Senator John M. Mead, who, though another Irish-Catholic, was identified with the Lehman-Roosevelt-Wagner faction of the Democratic Party and received the ALP nomination as well as that of the Liberal Party. Mead received ten times the percentage vote on these two tickets in the Second A.D. that he won in Richmond.

When, in 1950, Congressman John J. Lynch was nominated for Governor by the Democrats, the Liberal Party reluctantly endorsed him. Lynch had represented a Bronx district which included part of the Second A.D. Although he consistently talked like a conservative Irishman, he usually voted with the Fair Deal. Endorsement of him by the Liberal Party at least enabled many Jews to express their dissatisfaction with the conservative tendencies within the Democratic leadership in New York State. Lynch received fifteen times the percentage Liberal Party vote in the Bronx Second A.D. that he won in Richmond. In 1954 the Democrats nominated a liberal again, Averill Harriman, and the Jewish third party vote went down although 6,000 Jews in the Second A.D. preferred to vote for Harriman on the Liberal Party ticket rather than pull the Democratic lever.

The minor party proclivities of Jewish voters were most fully expressed between 1942 and 1954 because the Democratic candidates before and since have been liberals. As shown in the section on Presidential preference, the pattern of attraction and withdrawal of Jews to and from the Democratic Party depends on their perception of the Democratic nominees as liberals or conservatives. The pattern is similar in gubernatorial and mayoralty contests. When the Democratic candidate is liberal, Jews will vote for him on the

Democratic ticket or under a third party label if he has received minor party endorsement. If the Democratic nominee is conservative, many Jews will withdraw from the Democratic Party, vote Republican where they perceive the Republican aspirant as liberal enough, and, as is more often the case, vote for a left-wing minor party candidate when they feel the major parties offer them little choice.

MINOR PARTY VOTING IN STATE AND LOCAL CONTESTS IN BOSTON

The preponderance of Irish voters in the city of Boston makes impossible the development of minor parties comparable to the Liberal and American Labor Parties in New York. Thus, with rare exceptions, Boston voters have not had the opportunity to vote for non-Marxist radical or liberal minor party candidates for state and local office. However, the voters of Ward 14 have consistently turned in a higher percentage minor party vote for Governor than non-Jewish voters in other areas. Only in one year, 1936, was the percentage minor party vote higher in Irish Ward 15 than in Ward 14. Two right-wing party candidates, William McMasters of the Union Party, and Fred G. Bushold under the Union-Coughlin-Townsend label, were in the contest for Governor. Jewish voters could hardly be expected to vote for isolationist, anti-Roosevelt, anti-Semitic candidates, and only 280 votes were recorded in Ward 14 for McMasters and Bushold, two-thirds of these coming from the five least Jewish precincts in the Ward. In Ward 14 more votes were recorded for the Communist gubernatorial candidate, Otis Archer Hood, than for Messrs. Bushold and McMasters combined. But Bushold and McMasters ran well in Irish areas, even receiving seven per cent of the vote in middle-class Ward 15.

In Ward 14, minor party voting for Governor was strongest in 1930, 1932, and 1934. The minor party vote in each of these years represents the combined vote of the Socialist, Socialist Labor, and Communist Party candidates. The bulk of the minor party vote in these years went to the popular

Socialist candidate, Alfred Baker Lewis. In years of depression and ethnic tension, the old Socialist ties of Boston Jewry expressed themselves in considerable minor party activity. Actually the Socialist vote would have been higher in 1930 and 1932 in Ward 14 had not Jewish voters been presented with the extraordinary opportunity to vote for a liberal Democratic Protestant for Governor, James B. Ely. When the Democrats nominated James Curley in 1934, the Jewish Socialist vote went up accordingly.

In 1936, Jews were pulled back into the Democratic Party by the same gravitational force which drew many Irish Democrats into the Coughlin and Union Party folds. Since 1936 the Jews have been almost as unwilling to waste their votes on Communist and Socialist candidates as others, although they more often voted for a Marxist for Governor than for President.

In fact, there is a marked tendency for the Socialist and Communist vote to go up in Jewish areas as the office in contest diminishes in importance. For example, the vote for Marxist candidates for Governor, while greater than that given to radical candidates for President, is less than that given to Socialists and Communists aspiring to local offices.

MARXISTS VOTES FOR LOCAL OFFICE

The history of Otis Archer Hood, Dorchester sculptor and Chairman of the Massachusetts Communist Party, well illustrates the willingness of many Jewish voters in the Hub City to vote for Marxist candidates for local offices. Hood was the Communist candidate for Governor in 1936, 1940, and 1942. Only in 1936 did the Communists run their own candidate for President, Earl Browder. Hood ran considerably ahead of Browder in Ward 14, although Browder, of course, received a higher proportion of the vote in Jewish neighborhods than anywhere else.[9] While Hood fared much

---

9. Actually, Browder received 41.7% of his vote in the three most Jewish Wards in Boston. They are 14, 12, and 3 in that order. Ward 3 is really predominantly Italian, but in 1936 it still had a substantial Jewish minority.

better in Ward 14 than elsewhere in his quest for the Governorship, he did even better when he sought a school committee seat in 1941, 1943, 1945, 1947, and 1949.

As candidate for Governor he was never able to win more
than one per cent of the total vote in Ward 14. However, in
1941 he and Max Lerner, Communist candidate for the
United States Senate in 1930,[10] together received 27.9 per
cent of the votes recorded for all eighteen candidates for the
School Committee in Ward 14, while in the city as a whole
less than five per cent of the votes went to Hood and
Lerner.[11] In 1943 and 1945 Hood received 13.3 per cent and
14.5 per cent of the vote cast for School Committee candidates in Ward 14 in fields of seven and ten, more than
two and one-half times his strength in the city as a whole.
In a field of fifteen candidates in 1947 Hood received more
than five per cent of the votes cast, better than twice his
percentage in the entire city. In 1949 his popularity in Ward
14 actually increased, while it remained stable or petered out
in non-Jewish wards.

In other years the pattern has been similar. Marxist candidates for lesser offices do better than those contesting for
high office. In 1936 the Socialist candidate for the Senate,
the well-known Albert Sprague Coolidge, Professor of Chem-
istry at Harvard and subsequently Chairman of the Massachusetts Civil Liberties Union, while receiving a higher vote
in Ward 14 than anywhere else, ran behind Socialist candidates for minor offices.

Running far ahead of all Communist and Socialist candidates in 1936 (including Browder, Hood, and Coolidge) in
Ward 14 were the Socialist candidates for Clerk of the
Superior Court (Civil Business) and for Registrar of Probate and Solvency, Antoinette F. Konikow and John Brooks

---

10. Lest there be any mistake, this is *not* Professor Max Lerner of
Brandeis University, the author and teacher.

11. Since voters can choose more than one candidate in a School Committee election, a comparison between the percentage vote cast for Hood
as a gubernatorial aspirant and a School Committee candidate may be
misleading. The broad tendency to go Marxist for less important offices
is clear, however.

Wheelright. Konikow and Wheelright ran against John Patrick Connally and Arthur W. Sullivan, who received not only the Democratic designation, but Republican endorsement as well. In such contests the Socialist, anti-Tammany, anti-Irish, "good-government" propensities of Jewish voters make themselves felt. In Ward 14, Wheelright won 8.5 per cent of the vote cast for Registrar of Probate, two and one-half times as much as he received in any non-Jewish ward. Konikow won 12 per cent of the votes recorded in Ward 14 for Clerk of the Superior Court, three times the percentage vote given her in any Gentile ward.

It can nearly always be predicted that Socialist candidates for the unimportant offices will do better than the men who head the ticket. In 1926, for example, the candidates for Governor on the Socialist, Socialist Labor, and Workers (Communist) Party tickets could win only 3.5 per cent of the vote in Ward 14 while 15.5 per cent of the vote for Auditor went to candidates on the same slates, none of whom were Jewish. To choose another typical example, Socialist gubernatorial nominee Jeffery W. Campbell ran 13 per cent behind Saul Friedman, Socialist candidate for the City Council, in 1938.

There are four reasons why left-wing minor party candidates for relatively unimportant offices run ahead of candidates for Governor or Attorney General on the same ticket. One applies equally to all voters:[12] very often candidates for the City Council or the School Committee aspire to represent areas in which they themselves live and where they may have a strong personal following. The remaining three reasons apply only to Jewish voters. First, most Jewish voters in Dorchester and Mattapan (Ward 14), and for that matter in most big cities, do not feel committed to or involved in

---

12. Jewish voters are not alone in giving a higher percentage minor party vote to candidates for lesser offices. But what is significant is that the increase among Jewish voters is invariably substantially higher as the office becomes less important, despite the fact that Jews turn in the highest minor party vote for important offices to begin with. This is true in other cities as well as in Boston.

the regular Democratic organizations. Second, Democratic candidates for the big offices, for Governor and certainly for President, must have a much wider appeal than the Democratic candidates for local office, who are so frequently professional Irish politicians. Third, although the Jewish voters may be reluctant to hurt the chances for Democratic control of state government in order to keep less liberal Republicans out of power, they can express their dissatisfaction with conservatism in the Democratic Party and their wishes for a more progressive program by voting for minor party Marxist candidates for lesser offices.

LIBERALISM, INTERNATIONALISM AND
THE MINOR PARTY VOTE

Thousands of Russian Jews were Socialists for the first two decades of this century because of their belief in the Socialist programs calling for a welfare state (liberalism), international brotherhood (internationalism), and civic reform. When other minor parties emerged to press for elements of the old Socialist platform, they were received most favorably by Jews. The strong Jewish vote for LaFollette was a vote for the extension of governmental responsibility for social welfare. The powerful Jewish vote for Wallace was largely a vote for a continuation of wartime internationalist collaboration with Soviet Russia and the strengthening of the United Nations. The unusual Jewish response to LaGuardia resulted from the image which Jews had of the stumpy Mayor as an internationalist, New Dealer, and civic reformer all rolled into one.

Jewish minor party voting, like split-ticket voting and presidential preferences, during these past three decades has been largely the result of ethno-religious group norms and interests. Those norms and interests have worked in favor of the so-called "liberal" and "internationalist" candidates with very few exceptions.

CHAPTER XI

Sources of Jewish Internationalism and Liberalism

WHY INTERNATIONALISM?

ON NOVEMBER 3, 1942, the voters of four Boston wards went to the polls to vote on, among other things, the somewhat academic question of the formation of a democratic world government. It was hardly a surprise that the voters of Boston's second most Jewish ward were more enthusiastic about the idea of world government than voters elsewhere.[1] The reputation of the Jew for internationalism and cosmopolitanism, a reputation for which he has suffered much at the hands of both Hitler and the Communists, is well deserved. "Every influence and contact and experience has made him a universalist and an internationalist . . . he has participated out of proportion to his numbers in movements for international justice, understanding, and humanitarianism, and has been receptive to social philosophies with a world view such as socialism, communism, and a world state."[2] The wellsprings of Jewish internationalism are not hard to find.

The Jews, having been dispersed over the face of the globe for 2,000 years, have rarely been welcome or at home

---

1. Because of a quirk in referendum procedure, only four wards voted on the measure to call an international convention to write a world constitution. The results: Ward 5 (Yankee and upper-middle class) 73% approved; Ward 12 (Jewish and middle class) 82.3%; Ward 15 (Irish and middle class) 71.2%; Ward 20 (Irish-Yankee and upper-middle class) 66.8%.
2. J. O. Hertzler, "The Sociology of Anti-Semitism Throughout History," in Graeber and Britt, *op. cit.*, p. 76.

anywhere. First as traders, then as moneylenders, then as shopkeepers they were tolerated in the professions that were either too risky for Christians or prohibited to them. In these capacities Jews kept traveling and were in almost constant contact with one another. Consequently, the language, culture, folklore, and religion which the Jews developed are in many important respects transnational.

The modern state system has brought only occasional relief from persecution to the Jews. Since the seventeenth century, all European states have at some time or other sponsored anti-Semitic legislation as a matter of state policy. In the last eighty years anti-Semitism has increased rather than diminished—pogroms in East Europe, the Dreyfus affair, and more recently the monstrous persecutions of Hitler and Stalin. There have been periods of surcease from national, state-sponsored anti-Semitism. For the past 100 years no state-originated liabilities have been placed on Jews in English-speaking countries. Even the dictators Cromwell, Napoleon, and Peron in their own times eased the burdens placed on Hebrews in an effort to make them enthusiastic nationalists. But while Jews have become "good" Americans, Argentines, Frenchmen, and Germans, they are still not secure in the world of nationalism. They know that even liberal national states like the United States and France cannot prevent unofficial persecution. More importantly, they know from experience in Germany and Russia in recent decades that liberal national states cannot prevent the destruction of Jews as a people within illiberal states.

Consequently, American Jews are anxious that the United States, a country whose beneficence towards Jews in international affairs has been well demonstrated, play a strong role in international politics. At the same time they are anxious for the development and strengthening of the United Nations, and so they have taken an unusual interest in the U.N. genocide convention, the international bill of rights, and the strengthening of world organization generally.

WHY LIBERALISM?

The international history of the Jewish people, their cosmopolitan character, and their insecurity in a world of nation states may explain the extraordinary Jewish interest in the Marshall Plan, the U.N., and Point 4; but although the Jews are internationalists in matters of foreign policy, they need not be liberals at home. In 1940, the Poles were as strongly interventionist as the Jews. In 1944, Americans of Yankee stock tended to be strong supporters of the United Nations and the Anglo-American alliance. But Poles and Yankees divided on class lines on most New Deal issues, while the Jews did not. Why were the Jews liberals at home even after they had climbed to the top of the class ladder?

SOCIAL CLASS AND THE JEWS: A "VILIFIED
AND PERSECUTED MINORITY"

Such a question actually begs a prior issue. Were the Jews really perched on top of the class ladder, as alleged by national survey and area studies? In the Pope and Allinsmith studies already referred to, strictly objective criteria were used for measuring socioeconomic status, occupational prestige, education, and amount of income. In the Ward 14 study only occupational prestige and amount of income were used to index socioeconomic status. When W. Lloyd Warner and Leo Srole studied ethnic groups in "Yankee City" (Newburyport, Massachusetts), they rated ethnic groups in a class system based upon criteria concerning occupation, residence, and social class. They found that Jews had a much higher occupational prestige score than the natives (Yankees). But Jews as a group were not as high in social class as natives, and Jews did not live in as desirable neighborhoods as natives or Irishmen.[3] Even more importantly, Warner and Srole introduced the concept of subordination. The degree of subordination of an ethnic group was based upon the

3. W. Lloyd Warner and Leo Srole, *The Social Systems of American Ethnic Groups* (New Haven: Yale University Press, 1945), p. 96.

following five factors: (1) freedom of residential choice; (2) freedom to marry out of one's own group; (3) extent of occupational restriction; (4) access to associations, clubs, etc.; and (5) vertical mobility.

While the Jews were rated very high in the class system of Yankee City because that system gave great weight to such objective factors as amount of income and occupational prestige, the Jews rated very low in the system of subordination simply because of discriminations practiced against them. A hierarchy of six categories was established by the authors within the racial type "light caucasoid," and English-speaking Jews fell into the fifth category while European Jews fell into the sixth and last category.[4]

Such results confirm the findings of social distance tests. The results to these latter tests have not varied much since 1926 when Professor Emory S. Borgardus introduced them. Then, Professor Borgardus asked 1,725 Americans in a stratified sample to state their attitudes toward forty ethnic groups. German Jews ranked twenty-sixth from the top, Russian Jews twenty-eighth. Twenty years later the social distance scale was given to 1,950 persons in six different regions. This time Jews ranked twenty-third in a list of thirty-six ethnic groups. In another study of 1,672 white university students, Jews were rated fifth out of the nine ethnic groups being evaluated: native-born white, foreign-born white, Chinese, Indian, Jew, Filipino, Japanese, Negro, and Mexican in that order.[5] No matter how high Jews are placed on the socio-economic status or class scales which are based on occupation and income, they are unwanted by vast numbers of Christians. Although 16.3 per cent of the nation's medical doctors and 10.9 per cent of the nation's lawyers may be

---

4. *Ibid.*, p. 290.

5. This material is reported on and discussed in *Ethnic Relations in the United States* by Edward C. McDonagh and Eugene S. Richards (New York: Appleton-Century-Crofts, Inc., 1953), pp. 152-153. Another discussion of social distance scales may be found in *Groups in Harmony and Tension,* by Muzafer Sherif and Carolyn W. Sherif (New York: Harper & Bros., 1953), pp. 78-79.

Jews,[6] many Jews still cannot easily live where they want to, go to the schools of their choice, marry whom they please, or be respected for what they are.

It really matters little whether Jews are rated in a class system based on social distance tests and subordination or on occupational prestige in order to see that Jews as a group are made deeply insecure by the constant pressures of hostile Christian majorities. As Jean-Paul Sartre has put it, "An Israelite is never sure of his position or his possessions. He cannot even say that tomorrow he will still be in the country he inhabits today, for his situation, his power, and even his right to live may be placed in jeopardy from one moment to the next."[7] His feelings of insecurity are extensive.[8] Even in free and pluralistic America the Jews are engaged in a continuing quest for security. There are very few who do not sense that the security of the Jewish group depends in great measure upon the largesse of liberal government.

Since the Jews feel and know insecurity even when they are well-to-do and powerful, they are able to empathize with others who are discriminated against and insecure. It is no coincidence that the three books written since 1948 on the problem of legislation affecting Negro rights have been written by Jews.[9] Jews and Jewish organizations have always taken an extraordinary interest in Negro rights. One of the

---

6. McDonagh and Richards, *op. cit.,* p. 171.

7. Jean-Paul Sartre, *Anti-Semite and Jew,* translated by George W. Becker (New York: Schocken Books, 1948) , p. 132.

8. For studies which show psychological insecurity of Jews compared to non-Jews, see Abraham P. Sperling, "A Comparison between Jews and non-Jews," *Journal of Applied Psychology,* Vol. XXVI (1942) pp. 828-40; May Sukov and E. G. Williamson, "Personality Traits and Attitudes of Jewish and non-Jewish Students," *Journal of Applied Psychology,* Vol. XXII (1938) , pp. 487-92; Also Seward Keith and Meyer Freedman, "Jewish Temperament," *Journal of Applied Psychology,* Vol. XIX (1935) , pp. 70-84.

9. These three books are: Louis C. Kesselman, *The Social Politics of FEPC—A Study in Reform Pressure Movements* (Chapel Hill: The University of North Carolina Press, 1948) ; Monroe Berger, *Equality by Statute* (New York: Columbia University Press, 1952) ; Louis Ruchames, *Race, Job and Politics* (New York: Columbia University Press, 1953) .

reasons German Jewish immigrants were drawn to the newly formed Republican Party nearly one hundred years ago was that Party's stand on the slavery issue. Jews who had worn badges of slavery or inferiority for centuries were prone to sympathize with American blacks in their plight.

Knowledge of extreme persecution has made Jews acutely sensitive to the persecution of others. Moreover, Jews sense that inroads on the freedom and well-being of others may soon be followed by onslaughts on themselves. That is one reason why they have been in the forefront of civil liberties movements, and why their reaction to McCarthyism has been distinctly negative. It is difficult to imagine a large body of Catholic and Protestant clergymen representing *well-to-do* congregations *unanimously* passing a resolution denouncing Senator McCarthy and urging that his committee chairmanships be taken from him. Yet, this is just what the Conference of American Rabbis, representing 600 reform Rabbis in every section of the country, did in June 1954. The Rabbis also denounced the use of the term "fifth amendment communists" and protested the use of loyalty oaths. One Rabbi, probably repeating the thoughts of many Jews, compared McCarthy to Hitler.

Discrimination against Negroes and attacks on the civil liberties of others are felt by the Jews to be incipient attacks on them. Throughout history political and social reaction in other matters has been associated with persecution of the Jews, as Louis I. Newman has shown. And general authoritarianism has invariably brought anti-Semitism in its train.[10] In short, part of the explanation of Jewish liberalism must lie in the fact that anti-Semites are illiberal in political and social matters, as the authors of *The Authoritarian Personality* have shown.[11] If extreme anti-Semites tend to think

---

10. Louis Israel Newman, *Jewish Influence on Christian Reform Movements* (New York: Columbia University Press, 1925), p. 20.

11. T. W. Adorno, Else Frenkel-Brunswick, Daniel J. Levinson, and R. Nevitt Sanford, *The Authoritarian Personality* (New York: Harper & Brothers), Chapter 5.

strongly that Negroes ought to be segregated, that the government has no responsibility for the welfare of the people, and that free speech ought to be curtailed, Jews are not likely to agree with those views.

But this cause and effect relationship can also be turned on its head. Reactionaries may be anti-Semites because they think Jews are liberals. If that were true it would imply that Jews were liberals in matters of politics for other reasons besides their own group insecurity. It might signify that Jewish interest in the growth of the liberal state would exist even if the Jews were not "the most vilified and persecuted minority in history."[12] It may be that authoritarian Christians are anti-Semites because, as Maurice Samuel has insisted, they find the liberal and egalitarian implications of Jewish values intolerable.[13]

VALUES AND VOTES

Do Jewish group values tend to make the Jews liberals in the context of American politics? Some suggestive answers to this query come from a recent study on the cultural consciousness of Jewish youth. Its author, Werner J. Cahnman, asked questions of groups of Jewish and non-Jewish teenagers in an effort to discover the components of cultural consciousness in Jewish youth. Although he found that discrimination against Jews was a factor in the development of cultural consciousness, it was not the primary factor. Instead Cahnman concluded that "The primary twin elements of such consciousness are emotional nationalism (Zionism) . . . and humanitarian socialism."[14] Continuing, he wrote, "The sensitivity to discrimination among Jewish youth is increased

12. This is Justice Frankfurter's phrase from the opening of his dissenting opinion in the famous flag salute case, *West Virginia V. Barnette,* 319 *US* 624, pp. 646-647.

13. Maurice Samuel, *The Gentleman and the Jew* (New York: Alfred Knopf, 1950).

14. Werner J. Cahnman, "The Cultural Consciousness of Jewish Youth," *Jewish Social Studies,* Vol. XIV (July 1952), pp. 198-199.

because of the image of a just society which is at the back of their minds."[15] The Jewish teenagers were not only more concerned than their non-Jewish playmates about such things as race prejudice and the need for co-operation among minorities, but also about the infringement of civil liberties, the spread of militarism, and such problems as the unequal distribution of wealth and the need for minimum wage legislation. While such items as these last two, under the heading of "social abuse and social reform," were mentioned in 11.2 per cent of the Jewish replies, they were completely absent from the answers of the non-Jewish control group. One of the implications of the study is that Jewish "humanitarian socialism" is prior to discrimination against the Jews. The source of these attitudes lie not merely in a reaction to persecution, but in Jewish group values themselves.

Values are the criteria by which goals are chosen. If the Jewish youth Cahnman questioned actually had an image of a just society in the back of their minds (and the non-Jewish teenagers did not) even before they were treated unjustly, then the source of the Jewish attitude probably lies in Jewish values.

What are the distinctive values of America's Jewish subculture? To judge from a vast impressionistic literature and a growing systematic study of Jewish culture, those things most valued by Jews as Jews are: (1) Learning *(Torah)* ; (2) Charity *(Zedakeh)* ; and, for want of a better phrase or word, (3) Life's pleasures (non-asceticism) . In probably no other American subculture is so high a value placed upon learning and intellectuality, or upon the helping of the poor by the rich and the weak by the strong, or upon living a good life upon earth in full use of one's body. These three values, taken together or regarded separately, have helped to guide Jewish political behavior in recent decades along what in the discourse of our times would be called "liberal lines."

Learning (Torah) . The importance given to learning

---

15. *Ibid.,* p. 200.

and knowledge in the *Talmud* finds expression among contemporary Jewry in many ways. The learner, or student, or rabbi has always been given the highest status in Jewish community life. In a recent study of Polish Jewry it was found that the learner or student was still accorded the highest status in the community.[16] In this country settlement workers in immigrant quarters have always noticed the exceptional value which Jewish parents put on schooling for their children.[17] Talcott Parsons believes that intellectuality is the Jew's most distinguishing trait, and that "the strong propensity of the Jews to enter the professions can certainly, at least in part, be looked upon as a result of their traditional high regard for learning."[18] Albert Einstein similarly was convinced that any special notice which Jews may have won in intellectual endeavors is due "to the fact that the esteem in which intellectual accomplishment is held among the Jews creates an atmosphere particularly favorable to the development of any talents that may exist."[19]

The high value which Jews place on learning is also manifest in figures for Jewish attendance at colleges and universities and in the grades of Jewish students. In this country and in Europe the Jewish passion for learning results in unusually high attendance at the universities and similar centers of higher education. A recent study on college admissions in the United States shows that Jewish high school seniors are more anxious to continue their studies than their Christian classmates.[20] A veritable legion of studies

16. Mark Zborowski and Elizabeth Herzog, *Life is with People—The Jewish Little-Town of Eastern Europe* (New York: International Universities Press, 1953), Part III, Chapter I.

17. Frederick A. Bushee, *op. cit.*, p. 21. Robert A. Woods, ed., *The City Wilderness, op. cit.*, pp. 37, 232. Robert A. Woods, ed., *Americans in Process, op. cit.*, pp. 144, 353.

18. Talcott Parsons, "The Sociology of Anti-Semitism," in *Jews in a Gentile World*, ed. by Graeber and Britt, *op. cit.*, p. 106.

19. Albert Einstein, *Out of My Later Years* (New York: Philosophical Library, 1950), p. 250.

20. Morton Clurman, "How Discriminatory Are College Admissions?," *Commentary*, Vol. 15 (June, 1953).

show that Jewish boys and girls make better grades and achieve higher intelligence scores than non-Jewish students.[21] Such differences cannot easily be ascribed to differences in hereditary endowment, but can be explained by the strong value which is placed on learning and knowledge in Jewish culture.

Although Thorstein Veblen thought that the unusual "Intellectual Pre-eminence of Jews" would disappear after the establishment of a Jewish state, there is evidence of the continued emphasis which Jews put on learning for learning's sake. Even in Israel itself, many of the leaders of the government have in the past been noted for their scholarship and intellectual achievement.[22]

Charity (Zedakeh). The second in the important trilogy of Jewish values is *Zedakeh*, the Hebrew word for charity used in the *Old Testament* and the *Talmud*, and which is one of the few Hebrew words carried over into the Yiddish idiom. Of the three values, this one has the most relevance to the politics of our time. Its most precise meaning is not charity in the English sense of that word. Most students of Jewish community culture would agree that its real meaning is not charity but justice; "social justice" would be more accurate.

---

21. See the following: N. Nardi, "Studies in Intelligence of Jewish Children," *Jewish Education,* Vol. XX (1948), pp. 41-50. The I.Q. of Jewish children in New York was found to be much above the average of a non-Jewish control group regardless of home environmental factors.

E. Clark, "Motivation of Jewish Students," *Journal of Social Psychology,* Vol. XXIX (1949), pp. 113-117. In a study of 6,774 freshmen at Northwestern University it was found that Jewish students, especially the boys, received higher grades than non-Jews even when aptitudes as measured by aptitude tests were held equal.

L. M. Terman, *Genetic Studies of Genius* (Palo Alto: Stanford University Press, 1925), p. 648. At the time of his study Terman found twice the percentage of bright Jewish boys and girls as were found among Gentiles.

22. The first prime minister, Ben Gurion, was a student of Greek philosophy. His successor, Moshe Sharett, is an accomplished linguistic scholar. The first President, Chaim Weitzman, was a chemist of renown. Isaac Ben Zvi, now Israeli President, has been a scholar all his adult life. The Knesset is as packed with historians and economists as our Congress is studded with lawyers.

The heritage of *Zedakeh,* even though American Jews
may not be familiar with the word itself, is deeply rooted in
Jewish community life. In his chapter on the Jewish mind
Louis Wirth wrote, "The relation between the giver and the
receiver of charity was a peculiar one in ghetto society. Charity was more or less synonymous with justice, and to give to
the poor, the orphans, and the helpless was a religious
duty."[23]

To give is still a *mitzvah* (blessing) in Jewish community
life, and *Zedakeh* is still highly prized. In a recent and
well-received study of Jewish life in the towns of Eastern
Europe it was concluded that *Zedakeh* was valued only second to learning. As the authors wrote, "Praying three times
a day does not make you a Jew. You have to be a Jew for
the world. That means you have to do something for other
people as well."[24] In still another study of the value system
of East European Jews, Natalie Joff observes differences in
the traditional Western attitudes toward reciprocity and the
Jewish attitudes:

> For a society within the framework of the Western
> cultural tradition, East European Jewish culture ex-
> hibits a minimum of reciprocal behavior. Wealth, learn-
> ing, and other tangible possessions are fluid and are
> channeled so that in the main they flow from the
> "strong," or "rich," or "learned," or "older," to those
> who are "weaker," "poorer," "ignorant," or "younger."
> Therefore all giving is downward. . . .
> It is mandatory for the good things of life to be
> shared or to be passed downward during one's lifetime.
> . . . It is one of the greatest blessings in the world to
> put what you have at the service of others, be it wealth,
> learning, or children.[25]

---

23. Louis Wirth, *The Ghetto* (Chicago: University of Chicago Press,
1928) , p. 81.
24. Zborowski and Herzog, *op. cit.,* p. 230.
25. Natalie F. Joff, "Non-Reciprocity Among East European Jews," in
The Study of Culture at a Distance, edited by Margaret Mead and Rhoda
Metraux (Chicago: The University of Chicago Press, 1953) , pp. 386-387.

Although *Zedakeh* enjoins the individual Jew to help the weak and the poor, Jewish charity has been more than just alms-giving by individual benefactors. It has been considered part of the governance of the community itself. In some countries in the Middle Ages Jews "were obliged by law to provide for their poor, or were made jointly responsible for taxes or fines imposed on members of the community. . . . Thus, in the course of centuries, the support of the poor by the rich became a custom, a duty of the rich, and a right of the poor."[26] This tradition of corporate charity has been carried over into the philanthropic enterprises of English and American Jewry.[27]

In explaining the continuing solidarity of the Jewish people, Albert Einstein placed the Jewish respect for *Zedakeh* above everything else. Although he stated the proposition too strongly, there is a partial truth in his claim that "The bond that has united Jews for thousands of years and unites them today is above all, the democratic ideal of social justice, coupled with the ideal of mutual aid and tolerance among all men."[28]

Life's pleasures (non-asceticism). A third Jewish value which is frequently stressed in the literature on Jewish culture is probably best understood when put negatively. It is non-asceticism. As Rabbi Morris N. Kertzer writes, "Judaism does not accept the doctrine of original sin. . . . Nor do we consider our bodies and our appetites as sinful."[29] Jews place a high value on *a pleasureable life in this world.* Since Jews

---

26. Arthur Ruppin, *The Jews in the Modern World* (London: Macmillan & Co., Ltd., 1934), p. 352.

27. See Israel S. Chipin, "Judaism and Social Welfare," in *The Jews, Their History, Culture and Religion,* edited by Louis Finkelstein (New York: Harper & Brothers, 1949), Vol. 1, Chapter 16, p. 713; Boris Borgen, *Jewish Philanthropy* (New York: 1917); Ephriam Frisch, *An Historical Survey of Jewish Philanthropy* (New York: The Macmillan Company, 1924); Cecil Roth, *The Jewish Contribution to Civilization* (Cincinnati: The Union of American Hebrew Congregations, 1940), Chapter 12, "The Greatest of These is Charity."

28. Einstein, *op. cit.,* p. 249.

29. Morris N. Kertzer, "What is a Jew?", *Look,* June 17, 1952.

do not consider their bodily appetites as sinful, their behavior in matters of sex, drink, and food is affected accordingly.

In the Jewish villages of Eastern Europe "sexual enjoyment is considered healthy and good. . . . He [God] made man with sex organs and appetites, the exercise of them must be good."[30] Werner Sombart once compounded evidence on low rates of illegitimate Jewish births with quotations from the *Talmud* and *Bible* to argue that Jews were essentially ascetic in temper,[31] but he was very much mistaken. Jewish proscriptions are generally against the excessive use of bodily appetites, not against their use at all. And while it is true that Jews tend to have relatively few illegitimate children, the explanation lies partly in the widespread acceptance by Jews of birth control measures and their emphasis on sex within the marital relationship. For example, Kinsey found that American Jews have more marital intercourse than non-Jews at all age levels except the youngest.[32] Even more significantly, Kinsey and his associates reported that Jews talk more freely about sex than Christians.[33]

Though the Jew is temperate in matters of drink, as recent scholarship shows, the Jewish teetotaler is hard to find. The Jewish attitude toward the use of alcohol appears somewhat ambivalent. There is nothing the Jew despises in Christians so much as drunkeness, unless it is ignorance or stingyness. While the Jews loathe drunkeness, they do like to drink, especially sacramental wine. In fact, the Jews are enjoined to drink at various festivals and ceremonies. The Jewish attitude is not ascetic. It is well summed up in a colloquy which two young Jewish boys had in one of Angoff's novels as they watched Woodrow Wilson in a triumphal parade.

---

30. Zborowski and Herzog, *op. cit.*, p. 135.

31. Werner Sombart, *The Jews and Modern Capitalism,* translated by M. Epstein (London: T. Fisher Unwin, 1913), pp. 235-236.

32. Alfred Kinsey, *Sexual Behavior in the Human Male* (Philadelphia: W. B. Saunders, 1949), p. 492.

33. *Ibid.,* p. 496.

> Moshe and Kislov felt elated about Wilson. They
> were as excited as little boys.
> "I sometimes wonder," said Kislov, "what a man like
> Wilson does when he wants to rest, relax."
> Who knows? He doesn't drink, of that I'm sure,"
> said Moshe.
> "You don't mean never. A little Kidish [drink of
> sacramental wine] he no doubt has sometime," said
> Kislov.[34]

The Jewish attitude toward food is less restricted. Most
Jews are sensuous about food. There are few vegetarians
among them. In short, the Jewish spirit and temper are non-
ascetic because of the value which most Jews have always
placed on the enjoyment of life's pleasures.

JEWISH VALUES IN AMERICA

The question which comes to mind is: Are these values
of learning, *Zedakeh*, and life's pleasures Jewish values only?
Is not America a well-educated, charitable, and pleasure-
seeking society? While it is true that these things are valued
in American society, they are not the dominant values of our
Protestant-American culture as they are in Jewish culture.
According to Robin Williams there are four tests which may
be given to determine the importance of values in a culture.
Williams asks: What will people pay for? What do they pay
attention to? What do they reward and punish? What explicit statements of value do they make?[35] By all four tests it
is quite clear that learning, *Zedakeh,* and the enjoyment of
life on this earth are more valued by most Jews than by most
non-Jews. These values are more extensive, have lasted
longer, are sought and maintained with more intensity, and
bring more prestige to those who carry them in Jewish culture than in non-Jewish culture.

---

34. Charles Angoff, *In the Morning Light, op. cit.*
35. Robin Williams, *American Society* (New York: Alfred Knopf, 1952),
Chapter 11, "Culture Orientation in American Society." In the use of the
term "value" the writer relies heavily upon the discussion found in this
chapter by Williams.

So important are the love of learning and *Zedakeh* to Jewish tradition that the Jewish prayer book asserts that these two plus the worship of God constitute the three principal tenets of Judaism. It is true that there has been a passion for education in America which is unmatched in any other country in the world, but as Harold Laski has written, "It has been . . . an intensely pragmatic matter. . . ."[36] Whether or not it is true, as Laski asserts, that the American frontier tradition is responsible for the American stress on practical knowledge (life is the best education) there does exist in America a current of anti-intellectualism which runs alongside of the American public school tradition and which has found frequent expression in American politics in recent decades. While Americans generally disparage the "impractical" intellectual and academician, Jews tend to accord him the highest respect. It is fairly common for poor Jewish families to give a portion of their meagre savings to help support some bookish Rabbi who does nothing but study the *Talmud* in some dilapidated tenement. Such a man would probably be called a "waster" by most Christian Americans. It is the practical man who achieves status in America, the man who can build a better mousetrap or at least meet a payroll. That is why, for example, America's greatest scientific achievements are in the technological realm and not the area of pure science. It is why politicians can provoke a wry smile from most American audiences by a reference to "fuzzy-minded intellectuals." In America the passion for education has been hitched to America's drive to make things and do things. In the Jewish subculture the passion for learning stands on its own.

It is also true that charity and humanitarianism are respected in the United States. Americans readily pour millions of dollars into the heart fund, the polio fund, the tuberculosis association and similar charities every year. But

---

36. Harold Laski, *American Democracy* (New York: Viking Press, 1948), pp. 322 ff.

the Christian view of love (*Zedakeh*) as applied to politics has been considerably mitigated by the political implications of the Calvinistic notion that people get what they deserve, and that prosperity is a mark of moral virtue. The political influence of *Zedakeh* has also been curtailed by the impact of Social Darwinism on Protestant America. The idea that weakness or poverty is a mark of everlasting biological unfitness is contrary to the very essence of *Zedakeh*. Yet, William Graham Summner urged such an idea on Protestant America with considerable success. The notion that poverty, for example, is an index of biological and moral degeneration lent itself admirably to the defenders of the status quo for a half century after Appomattox. This is not to say that American society is not a charitable society. But charity is not generally accorded as a matter of right. The recipients of charity ought to "deserve" it, not merely need it.

As for non-asceticism, American society is no doubt getting more sensual too, as Max Lerner points out in a book on American civilization which will soon be published. Just how sensual American culture has become may be seen from the billions of dollars Americans spend on entertainment, cosmetics, food, labor-saving devices, and liquor (about eight million on liquor alone) each year. Still Christian America, particularly Protestant America, must contend with its bleak Puritan heritage. There is not the same free acceptance of physical pleasures that one finds in the Jewish culture. In fact, the case can be made that Jews have been disproportionately influential in the de-Puritanizing of America because of the special place of Jews in Hollywood, the legitimate theater, advertising, publishing, and the ladies' garment trades.[37] One student of culture conflict actually

37. For example, three of the eight principal movie companies are controlled by Jews. In three others Jews play a major role in management and ownership. Jews publish the magazine *Esquire,* which was the first important magazine of its type. The crimes at which Jews excel (the only crimes) according to crime statistics, are in the area of gambling and bookmaking. Jewish control of the ladies' garment industry and influence in advertising have no doubt helped to usher in the brassiere ads which may be found *ad infinitum* in our most respectable newspapers and magazines.

believes that the non-asceticism of the Jews and the asceticism of Gentiles has been the crucial difference and primary cause of tension between Hebrews and Christians in the United States. He concludes, "The areas of western European culture that have been colored by Protestant Christianity are essentially ascetic in temper; Jewish culture, on the other hand, is sensuous—good food, fine clothing, a fine home."[88]

THE POLITICAL IMPLICATIONS OF JEWISH GROUP VALUES

"Values are modes of organizing conduct—meaningful, affectively invested pattern principles that guide human action."[39] In what ways do Jewish values guide Jewish behavior in American politics? Considered separately, it is possible to see how each dominant value has had influence in shaping the Jewish position on issues and candidates in recent decades.

Zedakeh has more to do with politics directly than the Jewish love of learning and of life's pleasures. For *Zedakeh* deals with the distribution of power, which, after all, is what politics is about. In explaining the reverence of Jews for Franklin Roosevelt, Rabbi Ferdinand Isserman explicitly maintained that the Jewish *Zedakeh* was responsible. Of F.D.R. Isserman said:

> . . . he was partisan to protect, to uphold the rights of the weak. He did not lead for sympathy for the weak, he spoke of their rights. Judaism knew no charitable concept which meant that generosity and goodness of soul induces men to help the weak. It knew tsedokah, righteousness, not charity. Righteousness means the rights of men. It was said that Roosevelt was partial to the Negroes. So he was. They were the weak. . . . It was said that he sided with oppressed people. So he did. . . . Roosevelt shared the prophets' faith in the rights of the weak. . . .[40]

---

38. Graeber and Britt, *op. cit.*, p. 235.
39. Williams, *op. cit.*, p. 373.
40. Max Kleinman, *op. cit.*, pp. 72-73.

Zedakeh, as well as Jewish insecurity, would help promote Jewish sympathy for the Negro and help induce a favorable attitude toward progressive taxation, Roosevelt's war on the economic royalists, social security, and most of the programs which constituted the New Deal. It would also explain the favorable attitudes of Jewish businessmen and professional men toward an extension of power to labor, reported on in Chapter VII, as long as they thought of laborers as being relatively weak or underprivileged. It would also explain the results of the liberalism or altruism test given to the voters of Ward 14 in 1953, the much greater willingness of the Jewish voters to be taxed to aid the less fortunate in Kentucky or even in Africa and Asia.[41] *Zedakeh* would also explain why 62.7 per cent of the voters of Jewish middle-class Ward 14, and only 31 per cent of the voters of Yankee upper-middle class Ward 5, and 51.4 per cent of the electors in Irish middle-class Ward 15 in the city of Boston voted to give pensions to deserving citizens over sixty-five in 1942. It would explain why 76 per cent of the votes cast in Ward 14 in 1950 on the issue of raising the minimum wage were favorable as compared to only 47 per cent of those cast in Ward 5 and 74.5 per cent of the vote in Ward 15. It might even explain why 86 per cent of the voters in Ward 14 were in favor of absentee voting for disabled persons while only 76.6 per cent and 82.7 per cent of the electors in Ward 5 and 15, respectively, agreed when the question was put to a referendum in Boston in 1944. The enthusiastic Jewish response to the New and Fair Deals cannot be put down to Jewish insecurity alone, economic, psychological or otherwise. *Zedakeh,* a word which is probably unknown to the majority of American Jews, played its role in shaping Jewish political behavior in recent decades because of the structuring of political issues. It is difficult to see the relevance of *Zedakeh* to the silver-gold issue or the tariff issue, even

---

41. 56.9% of the Jews and 39.8% of the Christians agreed that they ought to help pay for the roads and education of people in Kentucky. 44.5% of the Jews and 28.9% of the Christians agreed that they ought to be taxed to help raise standards of living in Asia and Africa.

though germaneness might exist. But how quickly *Zedakeh* comes into play on such questions as unemployment compensation, shorter work, higher wages, relief, WPA, and so on.

The Jewish reverence for learning has also played a role in making the Jews political liberals in recent decades. It has influenced the Jewish response to individual candidates as well as to specific issues. In another of Angoff's novels, the ancient Jewish Alte Bobbe "was very pleased that Woodrow Wilson was elected President. She said, 'He has so much grace and learning. Ah, it's a wonderful country where a professor, a learned man like that, can become the head man.' "[42] It has already been shown how the intellectuality of even candidates for minor office, such as Gasper Bacon, the ex-Republican Lieutenant Governor of Massachusetts or ex-Governor Ely of the Bay State, disposed Jewish voters in their favor. The very learned and intellectual manner of Adlai Stevenson, reputed to have lost him votes among non-Jews, won approval among Hebrews. Twenty-two and one-half per cent of the reasons given by Jewish Stevenson voters in Ward 14 for preferring the Governor concerned his personality and his intelligence compared to only 13.8 per cent of the reasons given by Gentile Stevenson voters. One Jewish housewife remarked " Stevenson spoke so beautifully. He was so educated. But then Eisenhower was a college man too."

It was the Jewish love of learning and intellectuality which, at least in part, assured their positive response to the Roosevelt "brain trust." The idea of professors in government did not seem incongruous to them as it did to many Gentiles. For centuries they had been taught that the most learned men ought to run the affairs of the community. They were not repulsed by the notion of planning in government as were many of their fellow Americans. Charity, welfare requires planning. That is a Jewish tradition. If the state is to

---

42. Charles Angoff, *Journey to the Dawn* (New York: The Beechurst Press, 1951) , p. 419.

take an active role in assuring the welfare of its citizens, it ought to put the best brains to work planning how this will be done.

On still another important group of issues the Jewish value of intellectuality helped promote the "liberal" position among Jews. On civil liberties issues the Jews became fierce defenders of intellectual independence. While almost 12 per cent of the Jewish voters in the Ward 14 sample were in strong agreement that even Nazis and Communists ought to have free speech, not a single Gentile respondent was in strong agreement with that position. To be sure, the insecurity of the Jews prompts their anxiety about civil liberties, but the value which Jews place on knowledge plays a role as well.

The non-asceticism of the Jews has also influenced the general Jewish position on the political issues of our time. On certain questions such as the liquor question or the birth control issue, it is easy to see how the non-asceticism or this-worldliness of the Jews directly influenced their position. The value which Jews place on life's pleasures was responsible for relatively high anti-prohibition votes which the voters of Ward 14 recorded in twelve referendum votes on that issue since 1928. In all but two of those referendum contests the vote against prohibition was always higher in Jewish Ward 14 than in any other middle-class ward in the city, including the Irish wards. When the voters of Boston were asked through a referendum question if they favored the giving of birth control information by doctors to patients in need of it, the favorable vote in the Jewish wards was proportionately six times as high as it was in most Catholic areas, and higher than in Yankee Ward 5.

But how has the non-asceticism of the Jews helped to make them political liberals as that term has been used in recent decades? The answer is that by its emphasis on this-worldliness and the enjoyment of life here and now, Jews have been made more receptive to plans for a better life, for reconstructing society, for remaking man's environment, for socialism, for millennialism. Taken together with the other Jewish values of learning and *Zedakeh,* the non-asceticism of the Jews has, along with their insecurity, helped to produce a distinctive Jewish political style, a style which has characterized the liberal position in our time.

THE JEWISH POLITICAL STYLE

As Rabbi Philip Bernstein puts it in his popular book, *What the Jews Believe,* "The Jewish outlook is by its very nature optimistic, progressive, forward-looking. . . . It prods Jews constantly to strive for a better world, to be in the thick and at the front of movements for social reform. Even the very Jewish radical who may ignore his Jewishness is the product of its messianic fervor."[43] This outlook, a product of Jewish insecurity and the Jewish value system, constitutes a political style, an approach to the issues of social organization. Implicit in this style is the view that man and his environment are malleable, that he is much more the creator of history than its creature. Implicit, too, is the notion that man's enviroment and his polity are made for him. Implicit is a dynamic view of law, that it is changing and made for man. It is more than accident that three of the five great legal names which Americans associate with sociological jurisprudence are Jewish names: Brandeis, Cardozo, and Frankfurter. (The others are Stone and Holmes.) And especially implicit in such a style is the belief that what happens in this life on this earth is very important, what happens here and now matters very much.

CHRISTIAN EMPHASES

Contrast this view with that which the Christian theologians Bernard I. Bell and Rheinhold Neibuhr assert is the orthodox Christian position. Bell raises the question, "But is man capable of getting better and better by his own

---

43. Philip S. Bernstein, *What the Jews Believe* (New York: Farrar, Straus and Young, 1950) , p. 419.

natural development or is he doomed to failure unless God intervenes? It makes a great deal of difference which of these alternatives is correct, a difference not only in theoretical doctrine but also in one's attitude toward living, one's source of hope and happiness, in social action, too."[44] Christianity has been split in its answer to this question. Judaism has not. Orthodox Christianity stresses the concept of redemption only through God's intervention. In recent years the Neo-Calvinists have lamented the failure of Christians to hold fast to this fundamental theological tenet. They have insisted that any departure from the Christian emphasis on complete dependence on God for the betterment of his condition has led to what Bell calls "the exaggerated optimism about man which . . . is the chief cause of our decay."[45] The failure of too many Christians to adopt what Niebuhr calls "Christian realism" in understanding man's sinfulness, his egocentricity, and utter helplessness without God has in his judgment led Americans too often into the fallacies of communism and utopian ideas for world government.[46]

But the fact is that American Jews, not Christians, have served these causes far out of proportion to their numbers. The Neo-Calvinists have exaggerated the political effects of liberal and heretical Christianity. After all, the vast majority of Christians still believe that man is stained with original sin and cannot be redeemed without God's grace. When the American sociologist, Lester Ward, stressed that man's power over nature was unlimited he was rejected, while the ideas of William Graham Summner dominated the thinking of the Supreme Court for more than forty years. Dependence on God for the improvement of man's condition has been coupled in the orthodox view with the idea that faith and repentance—not works—brings redemption. Of course, many

---

44. Bernard I. Bell, *Crowd Culture* (New York: Harper & Brothers, 1952), p. 111.

45. *Ibid.*

46. Rheinhold Neibuhr, *Christian Realism and Political Problems* (New York: Charles Scribner's Sons, 1953). See Chapters I and II and p. 183.

Christians have stressed works too, and it is impossible to speak of a single Christian position on any of these issues— so various and individualistic is Christian theology. The Catholics have had a long tradition of working among the poor, and in recent decades there have been many labor priests and waterfront priests, backed by Papal encyclicals, active in movements for social and economic reform. In the United States they have been joined by the followers of the Social Gospel movement led by Washington Gladden and Walter Rauschenbush. From the Social Gospel and similar movements came a Protestant emphasis on secularizing religion, on work in settlement houses, recreation centers, adult education, and political reform. Quaker concern has always manifested itself in humanitarian works. In the late nineteenth and early twentieth century, "liberalism" stressing the goodness of man, works, and social action was an important theological current running through all of the major Protestant denominations. It would certainly be a mistake to underestimate the role of liberal and secular Christianity in American life.

But it would also be a mistake to exaggerate it. While a number of Catholic leaders have been in the forefront of social action on behalf of the oppressed, Catholic law teaches resignation and moderation to the poor. Catholic Church leaders in the United States have been militantly anti-Socialist. More important than the Catholic political mood are the Protestant influences on American politics. The only major Protestant movement which has been optimistic about man and stressed his powers to improve life through social and political action has been the Social Gospel.

From the Anabaptists to the Fundamentalists, the political implications of the important Protestant theological movements, with the exception of the liberal "heresy" of the nineteenth century, have been conservative. Calvinism, Lutherism, Puritanism, Evangelicalism, Fundamentalism, and contemporary neo-Calvinism—all have tended to oppose the notion of social betterment through the state. Indeed, the Anabaptists reluctantly admitted that the state was necessary at all, and refused to assume any responsibility for it. Lutherans and Calvinists stressed the sinfulness of man. Crucial to the early Anglican position was the concept of justification through faith. Puritanism, which influenced all of the major Protestant denominations to some extent, emphasized asceticism. Fundamentalism has usually meant extreme social conservatism and suspicion of scientific and secular influences. The Evangelical movement in the first half of the nineteenth century insisted on the sinfulness of man, salvation through faith, and the need for conversion.

It is true that many of the leading evangelists were busily engaged in the front lines of various reform movements during this period, but these movements were usually aimed at the suppression of personal vice and immorality. They had nothing to do with the role of the state in society. Almost every single one of the leading evangelists opposed Andrew Jackson while supporting Sabbatarianism, temperance, and anti-slavery. In their theological writings Lyman Beecher, Charles Finney, Calvin Colton, Albert Barnes, and other evangelists showed considerable innovation, but they were politically conservative to a man. They worried over the souls of the poor but opposed poor relief, limitations on child labor, and extensions of the suffrage.[47] In fact, the great *theological radicals* (in their day) who have had the largest influence on American Protestantism—Calvin, Luther, and Wesley—were, unlike the Hebrew prophets of ancient times, *politically conservative.*

Surely, the Quakers and the Unitarians have been influential in American life; but who would argue that Quakerism has played a larger role in shaping American politics than Puritanism, or that a handful of Unitarians have had the impact of a movement such as Fundamentalism, which dominates whole sections of the country! Quaker concern

---

47. For a complete discussion of the evangelical movement in the North see Charles C. Cole, Jr., *The Social Ideas of the Northern Evangelists,* 1826-1860 (New York: Columbia University Press, 1954).

may make Herbert Hoover a great private humanitarian, but other influences determine his politics.

Still, it will be said that Christian liberalism must have had considerable impact if only to judge by the violent reactions of the Fundamentalists and Neo-Calvinists. It did have a large impact, but its influence was mainly theological and not political. The debate between liberals and fundamentalists was primarily over such matters as biblical criticism and the deity of Christ. Liberal theology reached its zenith during the early decades of the twenties, the very years when conservatism dominated American politics. Liberal theology at least implied that a truly Christian society could be achieved here on earth, but not necessarily through social action. For example, one way of exercising Christian responsibility was through individual "stewardship." This did not mean taking literally Jesus' extreme denunciation of wealth, but it did mean that the wealthy Christian should part with some of his money through philanthropy. But charity, like exploitation, was not the concern of the state, and the Christian theory of stewardship bears no resemblance to *Zedakeh*.

While liberal theology did not necessarily mean liberal politics, it sometimes did. Individual Quakers such as John Howard who struggled for prison reform and William Wilberforce who fought slavery were indeed motivated by religious force. Horace Buschnell and Washington Gladden stressed the social implications of Christianity. The Social Gospel was "a new application of the Christian ethic to the demands of a new historical situation"—the industrial age.[48] In fact, many theologians stressed the teachings on social justice of the Hebrew prophets Amos and Micah. But unlike Amos and Micah, the Christian liberals did not demand a recasting of society. Most of them only hoped to make life more bearable on earth, and for a great many the emphasis

48. John Dillenberger and Claude Welch, *Protestant Christianity* (New York: Charles Scribner's Sons, 1954), p. 245.

was still on the world to come. Even Wilberforce preached to the impoverished to accept their lot in life, and Rauschenbusch never supposed that the kingdom of God could be produced by man's efforts. The Social Gospel was a popular movement in the United States for fifty years from 1870 through 1920, but it appears to have affected American politics only slightly throughout its growth. It reached its height in 1908 when it was symbolized by the organization of the Federal Council of the Churches of Christ in America. Ironically, that was the year William Howard Taft, a Unitarian and the candidate of the conservatives, defeated fundamentalist theologian and "liberal" politician William Jennings Bryan for the Presidency.

The optimism of the liberal theology of the late nineteenth century has fallen into disrepute in the aftermath of the great depression, genocide, two degrading world wars, and the terrors of world communism. The Neo-Calvinist writings of Reinhold Niebuhr, J. V. Langmean Casserly, and others have re-emphasized the traditional Christian view of sinful man and its insistence that faith is the key to salvation. There can be little doubt that the Christian emphasis on faith and repentance as contrasted with the Jewish stress on works has influenced American political behavior. As one Jewish writer recently pointed out, faith is essentially personal and works are inherently social.[49] Contrast the recent urging of the executive director of the Rabbinical Assembly of America to Rabbis to raise questions and criticize social institutions with the oft-held Lutheran position that Christ's kingdom is not of this world, "and that therefore it is the preacher's duty to preach repentance and faith and not to concern himself with worldly affairs."[50] Because faith is personal and works are usually social, the Christian efforts at social and economic reform, great as they have been, have

---

49. Joseph R. Narot, "Judaism, Christianity, and Salvation," *The Reconstructionist*, Vol. XX (April 23, 1954), p. 16.

50. William Warren Sweet, *Religion in the Development of American Culture*, 1765-1840 (New York: Charles Scribner's Sons, 1952), p. 38.

been dwarfed by the energies which Christians have spent on the saving of souls. Enormous Christian effort goes into missionary work and pastoral counseling, while the Jews hardly pay any attention to these affairs at all. Catholics place strong emphasis on the confessional. And the Church is prepared to make its peace with any social order, authoritarian as well as democratic, so as to concentrate on its main job of personal salvation.

Because of the orthodox stress on the sinfulness of man and the necessity of faith for redemption, many Christians view as the greatest of all impieties any effort by man to bring about what God has promised. Thus, Arnold Toynbee has criticized the restoration of the state of Israel as a prideful usurpation of Divine Will. For the same reason the English historian, like many Neo-Calvinists, has termed the communist movement a "Christian heresy" because it strives to produce the kingdom of God on earth without God, thus denying the capacity of the Almighty to do the task alone. But if the communist movement is in a sense a Christian heresy, it is also Jewish orthodoxy—not the totalitarian or revolutionary aspects of world communism, but the quest for social justice through social action.

Although there are many exceptions, Jews have tended to emphasize the interrelatedness of religion with social organization, while numberless Christians have believed that their temporal interests could be divorced from their religious convictions. By comparison with the Jews the Christians have been otherworldly. Contrast, for example, the notion held by many Christians that celibacy (as sharp a break from this world as one can make) is the highest form of life with the view which Rabbi Bernstein says Jews hold— that "The reward of the good life is the good life."[51] Undoubtedly, there are hundreds of thousands of Christians

51. Bernstein, *op. cit.*, pp. 4, 65. Writes Bernstein (p. 4) "Most Jews have assented to the judgment of an olden Rabbinic teacher who [said] . . . 'One hour of repentance and good deeds in this world is better than the whole life of the world to come.'"

who agree with Bernstein and his coreligionists, but there are also hundreds of thousands who do not. In a recent book on Christianity and social problems, H. Ralph Higgens describes three typical Christian approaches to social questions, not one of which is held by any sizable number of Jews.[52] The first he calls the "hands off view." Injustice and suffering are to be endured since they are unavoidable "and are to be used by the Christian as spiritual musclebuilders." The second is the "first aid kit approach" used to salve the wounds of an unjust social order. The third holds that nothing much can be done until all men have been converted. Each of these views, as Higgens points out, is melancholy and based on a concept of selfish man. The fact that these are not the only Christian views is borne out by Higgens' own plea for Christian action on social problems, stressing the relevance of Christian morality to social life in the tradition of liberal theology.

The main point is that while there are many Christian approaches to social and political questions, the Jewish position has been relatively unified. While orthodox Christianity stresses man's sinfulness, repentance, and otherworldliness, the Jews appear to have emphasized man's potentialities, works, and life here and now. Orthodox Christian theology has tended to color American politics with a conservative cast from which Jews have been largely exempt. On the other hand, Jewish cultural and theological values have promoted a liberal and radical political style.

It cannot be urged too often that there are many exceptions to the general tendencies described above. Thousands of Methodists, Episcopalians, Presbyterians, Baptists, and Catholics to say nothing of Unitarians and Quakers are, in Bernstein's words, "optimistic" in politics, "strive for a better world," and are "in the thick . . . of movements for social reform." But tendencies there are, and among Jews aggres-

---

52. H. Ralph Higgens, *Christianity and America's Social Problems* (New York: Comet Press, 1952), p. 8.

sive and optimistic reformism in politics is found much more often than among their Christian countrymen.

None of this is to say that Christian theology is responsible for making America conservative. In fact, just the opposite is true. The United States is a liberal-democratic state, and the Judeo-Christian emphasis on love, justice, and human dignity is in no small measure responsible for democracy itself. But there is a conservative position within the framework of American politics which can be categorized by such notions as the importance of order, the sanctity of private property, the futility of social change, and the Herbert Hoover type of rugged individualism. These elements of conservatism in American politics may be mainly secular in origin, but they meet with little resistance from the major strains of Christian theology and with a great deal of opposition from Jewish cultural and theological values.

JEWISH SOLIDARITY IN POLITICS

Accepting the view that Jewish insecurity and the Jewish value system primarily account for the political liberalism of American Israelites in recent times, the query remains, "Why do Jews take their values and norms from the ethno-religious group they belong to in making political judgments? Why don't they relate their political behavior to the norms of other reference groups they belong to, their class groups or occupational groups?

Like all of us, Jews relate to many reference groups.[53] Jewish doctors may adopt either Jewish norms or those of the AMA in judging proposals for socialized medicine; Jewish lawyers may adopt Jewish norms in judging the use of the Fifth Amendment by crypto-communists or they may

---

53. I have accepted the definition of the Sherifs that reference groups are "simply those groups to which the individual relates himself as a part or to which he aspires to relate himself psychologically." *Op. cit.*, p. 161. For a discussion of reference group material see Theodore Newcombe, Eugene L. Hartley, and others in *Readings in Social Psychology* (revised edition; New York: Henry Holt & Co., 1952), Part IV, B.

use those of the American Bar Association; Jewish taxpayers may employ Jewish values as points of reference for judging tax legislation or they may follow the views of a taxpayer's association. The evidence presented in the preceding chapters shows that an unusual number of Jews do derive their political attitudes and opinions from being Jewish. It is that which makes them political liberals and internationalists. Why is it that membership in the Jewish group, apparently without regard to the depth of one's involvement in that group, is so vital in determining the vote behavior of Jews?

There are basically two answers to this, and one of them has already been provided. The Jewish religion and culture are centered on the here and now as the Christian religions and cultures are not. And there is evidence that younger Jews believe that the Jewish religion should become less and less concerned with theology and ritual and more and more concerned with secular social and economic problems.[54] But the fact that Judaism is this-worldly does not mean that Jews will apply Jewish norms to worldly affairs in competition with other norms.

The main answer lies in the unusual cohesiveness and solidarity of the Jewish group. Through centuries of dispersion, persecution, and even genocide the Jews have persisted as a people. The Jews have survived because of the extraordinary will to survive. They have resisted conversion, eschewed intermarriage, and scorned suicide. In the ghettos they developed a strong feeling of common responsibility. Perhaps more than anything else it was the ghetto experience which produced cohesiveness among the Jews. As Louis Wirth explained in his monumental study on Jewish ghetto life:

> What makes the Jewish community—composed as it
> is in our metropolitan centers of so many heterogeneous
> elements—a community is its ability to act corporately.

---

54. Meyer Greenberg, "The Jewish Student at Yale," in *Race Prejudice and Discrimination, op. cit.*, p. 317. Nathan Goldberg, "Religious and Social Attitudes of Jewish Youth in the U.S.A.," *Jewish Review*, Vol. 1 (December 1943) , pp. 139-141.

It has a common set of attitudes and values based upon common traditions, similar experiences, and common problems. In spite of its geographical separateness it is welded into a community because of conflict and pressure from without and collective action within. The Jewish community is a cultural community. It is as near an approach to communal life as the modern city has to offer.[55]

Wirth wrote in 1928, when the American ghettos were beginning to disintegrate and the flow of orthodox Jews into the ghettos had just about stopped. But the spectre of anti-Semitism came to replace these unifying factors and to prevent the divisive effects of assimilation. Anti-Semitism made considerable headway in the 1920's and 1930's. Exclusion from good housing and better residential areas was extended. The quota system at schools, in professions, and in clubs barred Jews from access to influence and prestige. Then the depression and the rise of Hitler exacerbated tensions between Jew and Gentile. Over 100 anti-Semitic organizations sprouted during the 1930's, and Gerald L. K. Smith, Father Coughlin, and Gerald Winrod applauded Hitler's attempts to destroy European Jewry. The solidarity of the Jews was reinforced by these events, and the tight cohesiveness of American Jewry was assured for at least a few decades. Jewish doctors, lawyers, laborers, peddlers—all were made conscious of their Jewishness whether they wanted it or not. Their insecurity as Jews served to emphasize Jewish values as points of reference for political action. After the war the growth of Zionism in the United States reinforced cohesiveness still further. The total membership in Jewish voluntary organizations grew from 807,000 in 1935 to 1,085,000 in 1941 and 1,436,000 in 1945, a much higher rate of increase than for all voluntary associations in the United States.[56] Membership in nonpolitical organiza-

55. Louis Wirth, *op. cit.,* p. 279.

56. Leo Bogart, *The Response of Jews in America to The European Jewish Catastrophe,* 1941-1945, Unpublished M.A. Thesis, University of Chicago, 1948, p. 46.

tions such as the Workmen's Circle remained stable, but membership in Jewish political groups grew by leaps and bounds. Meanwhile, Jewish charities received a sudden burst of support which went far beyond the average national increase despite the fact that the ghettos in the big cities continued to disband and circulation figures for the Yiddish press went steadily down.

The events of our time have not only promoted Jewish unity, but they have made the Jews the most politicized group in the United States. During most of the nineteenth century American Jews were relatively indifferent to politics. Apathy resulted partly from a lack of issues which interested Jews, partly because Jews were so busy doing other things, and partly because of the reluctance of Sephardic and German Jews to enter politics as such. While Rabbinical sermons in the twentieth century are highly secular, mid-nineteenth century Rabbis generally objected to what they called "politics in the pulpit."[57] The Jewish pulpit was usually silent on such topics as free trade, labor unions, and governmental relief. Today, leading Rabbis speak out boldly on almost every major political question. The anti-Semitism and Zionism of recent decades have promoted group consciousness, which, in turn, has made Jewish values influential in shaping the political behavior of American Jews.

There are other contributing sources of Jewish liberalism, but they are probably not of major significance. Lewis Browne has forcefully stated the proposition that Jews are liberals and radicals in politics because they are an urban people.[58] American Jews are concentrated in the urban centers, but many of them were village and peasant folk in East Europe before they came to America. And the fact remains, within the cities other groups are sharply divided in politics on economic class lines whereas the Jews are not.

57. Robert I. Kahn, *Liberalism as Reflected in Jewish Preaching in the English Language in The Mid-Nineteenth Century*, Ph.D. Thesis, Hebrew Union College, 1949, p. 71.

58. Lewis Browne, *How Odd of God* (New York: The Macmillan Co., 1934), Chapter VI, especially pp. 216-222.

A PERSONAL CONCLUSION

Some readers may object that I have asserted the liberalism of the Jews and discussed the sources of Jewish liberalism in too sweeping a manner. Need it be said that there are thousands, perhaps hundreds of thousands of American Jews who are not liberals? Of course there are Jewish reactionaries, but these are the exceptions. Still, it ought to be remembered that this book is about Jews in a specific place and a specific time, and that even in a few short years these generalizations may fall. I should not like to be caught in the position of the great German sociologist, Werner Sombart, who wrote emphatically in 1913 that the intellectualism and lack of sensuousness in the painting of the Jews was proof of their asceticism—at the very time the Jewish Pissaro, Soutine, and Modigliani were putting brushes to canvas.

It may be that Jewish liberalism and internationalism are on the wane, and that the Jewish political style is less often found than it was fifteen years ago. The latter seems especially true. But in recent years, as during the first twenty years of the Republic, American Jewry has taken the liberal position in politics, and generalizations about the causes of Jewish liberalism ought not to be abandoned merely because they are large. Since they seem to be true, I would happily acquiesce in Albert Einstein's judgment that "Abandonment of generalization [in the field of politics] . . . means to relinquish understanding altogether."[59]

---

59. Einstein, *op. cit.*, p. 252.

APPENDIX

Methodological
and
Bibliographical Notes

CHAPTERS 2, 3, 4

THE MATERIALS and methods used in these chapters are essentially those of the historian. Chief reliance was placed upon encyclopedias, newspapers and periodicals, autobiographies and memoirs, and community histories.

ENCYCLOPEDIAS AND DOCUMENTARY HISTORY

For useful portraits of communities and personalities discussed in these chapters, refer to the *Jewish Encyclopedia,* 12 vols. (New York, 1901-1906) and the *Universal Jewish Encyclopedia,* 10 vols. (New York, 1939-1943). Of high value were volumes one to 40 of the *Publications of the American Jewish Historical Society.* Useful collections of documents may be found in Cyrus Adler and Aaron Margalith, *With Firmness in the Right, American Diplomatic Action Affecting Jews, 1840-1945* (New York: American Jewish Committee, 1946) and Morris U. Schappes, *A Documentary History of Jews in the United States, 1654-1875* (New York: The Citadel Press, 1950).

NEWSPAPERS AND PERIODICALS

These can be a gold mine for a researcher in political history. Various publications are referred to in the footnotes. Of principal service were the *American Hebrew* (1879-   ), the *Jewish Tribune* (1903-1931), the *Occident and Jewish Advocate* (1843-1868), and the *Jewish Advocate* (1902-   ).

MEMOIRS AND AUTOBIOGRAPHIES

There are a half dozen to a dozen volumes which offer some useful material on Jewish political history, but these books usually tell much more about an individual than they do about political behavior in a community. Typical selections are: Sol Bloom, *The Autobiography of Sol Bloom* (New York: G. P. Putnam's Sons, 1948) ; Emanuel Celler, *You Never Leave Brooklyn* (New York: John Day & Co., 1952) ; *Sixty Years in Southern California, 1853-1913,* edited by Maurice H. Newmark and Marco R. Newmark (New York: The Knickerbocker Press, 1916) ; Henry Morgenthau, *All in A Lifetime* (Garden City: Doubleday Page & Co., 1922) ; and Oscar S. Straus, *Under Four Administrations* (Boston: Houghton Mifflin Co., 1922).

COMMUNITY HISTORIES

Of considerable value in studying history of this kind are the many community histories which have been done. Among the best are: Samuel P. Abelow, *History of Brooklyn Jewry* (Brooklyn: Sheba Publishing Co., 1937), Chapter IV, "The Jews in Politics"; E. Milton Altfeld, *The Jews Struggle for Religious and Civil Independence in Maryland* (Baltimore: M. Curlander, 1924) ; Barnett R. Brickner, *The Jewish Community in Cincinnati,* Unpublished doctoral dissertation, (The University of Cincinnati, 1933) ; Herbert T. Ezekiel and Gaston Lichtenstein, *The History of the Jews of Richmond* (Richmond: Herbert T. Ezekiel, 1917) ; Hyman Grinstein, *The Rise of the Jewish Community of New York* (Philadelphia: The Jewish Publication Society of America, 1945) ; Louis Ginsburg, *History of the Jews of Petersburg, 1789-1950* (Petersburg: 1954) ; Charles Reznikoff, *The Jews of Charleston* (Philadelphia: The Jewish Publication Society of America, 1950) ; Stuart E. Rosenberg, *The Jewish Community of Rochester 1843-1925* (New York: Columbia University Press, 1954) ; and Leon L. Watters, *The Pioneer Jews of Utah* (New York: American Jewish Historical Society, 1952).

PUBLISHED ELECTION RETURNS

By the turn of the century enough Jewish immigrants had concentrated in the big East Coast cities to constitute a majority of the population in certain wards and assembly districts. I used the published election returns for the cities of Boston, Chicago, and New York to describe the vote behavior of Jews in those cities.

CHAPTER 5

It is to the wards and precincts that one must go to study the contemporary political behavior of any ethnic group such as the Jews. Only in the smallest electoral units are Jews clustered in sufficient numbers to make it possible to say of one area or another, "that is a Jewish ward, or that is a Jewish assembly district." Unless specified otherwise, I never have written of a "Jewish" ward or precinct unless the Jews constituted at least sixty-five per cent of the population of the area discussed. It is impossible to be precise about the percentage concentration of Jews in an area at a given time, but it is possible to approximate that concentration within a five or ten per cent margin of error. Expert population studies are the best guides for determining just how Jewish an area is. In many middle-sized cities the Jewish communities conduct their own censuses. Sometimes it is necessary to rely on the advice of local newspapermen, politicians, and religious leaders checked by voters' lists or similar directories.

Of course, high population mobility means that some wards which were heavily Jewish are no longer so. Although Jews constituted a large majority of the population in Paterson's Ward 4 twenty years ago, they are in the minority there today. Whereas Paterson's Ward 11 was non-Jewish ten years ago, it is now substantially Jewish. Jews are moving out of Ward 13 in Cincinnati, Ward 12 in Hartford, Wards 25 and 27 in Cleveland, for example, and are moving into Districts 28, 29, and 30 in Miami Beach. Another problem for the researcher is that redistricting changes the boundaries of wards and precincts overnight. After redistricting in New York in 1944, the 17th, 19th, and 21st Assembly Districts in New York County were no longer the most Jewish assembly districts there.

Despite the difficulties, it is important to find electoral units in which the percentage composition of the group being studied has been high for a long period of time. Students of electoral behavior know the grief that comes to those who attempt analysis and prediction on the basis of a very short time series. It is also wise to compare Jewish units with Polish or Irish or Italian units *in the same city*. In that way certain other factors which influence the vote can be controlled, such as the economic condition of the neighborhoods and political organization in the area. That is why I have often compared Jewish Ward 14 in Boston to Ward 5 (Yankee), Ward 15 (Irish), and Ward 3 (Italian), and also why I have frequently compared the Second Assembly District in the Bronx (Jewish) to Richmond County (Gentile) in New York City. All of these areas have been more or less ethnically homogeneous for a long period of time. The basic boundary lines of Ward 14, for example, have not changed since 1924. Irish Ward 15 is a particularly good unit for comparison because the average monthly rent, average value of one-dwelling-unit structures, and other crucial economic indices are practically identical with Ward 14. That is one reason why Richmond and the Bronx Second A.D. are good areas to compare. Census reports for monthly rent and annual income show practically identical median figures for these two areas.

The economic condition of wards and sometimes of precincts can be discovered by determining which census tracts lie within ward boundaries. That is done by simply superimposing census tract areas over ward boundaries on a ward map. The Department of Commerce, Bureau of the Census, publishes vital information on population, housing, and other matters for census tract areas based on the decennial census.

Election results for many cities may be obtained from the published election returns for those cities. In some cases, such as in Chicago, election returns for wards and precincts are not published, but they will be given out by the election commission for academic purposes. Where a visit to an election commission is not possible, the back file of a newspaper may provide the information needed.

LIMITATIONS ON THE USE OF AGGREGATE RETURNS

There are three basic limitations on the usefulness of aggregate returns for studies of this kind. They are: first, the context and climate of political decision varies from city to city even in Presidential elections; second, a study only of aggregate returns precludes analysis of the behavior of those Jews who live dispersed as small minorities in Gentile areas; and third, it is impossible to break down the returns for the entire population of a ward by subgroups.

The first two limitations are not insurmountable. It is true that the politics of any ethnic group in any city reflects to some extent the context of political life in that city and in the state or region in which the city lies. Group leadership, organizational strength, and political history are factors which vary in Jewish communities (as they do in other communities) from city to city. But familiarity with the local political conditions of a number of cities will help overcome this pitfall. Such familiarity would prevent the drawing of too broad an inference from the Jewish vote in Chicago in 1936, when Illinois had a Jewish New Deal Governor, for Jews elsewhere, say in Boston, where some of the Democratic leaders were avowed Coughlinites.

It is also true that aggregate returns cannot be used to study the political behavior of Jews in New Rochelle, New York or Muncie, Indiana, because such returns cannot tell how Jews voted in predominantly Christian areas. In the case of the Jews, however, this limitation is hardly conclusive since they are an overwhelmingly urban group. Seventy five per cent of America's Jews live in its five biggest cities, compared to only 12.5 per cent of the total U. S. population.

The third limitation on the use of aggregate returns is impossible to compensate for except through the use of other methods. Aggregate returns hide information about subgroups. A study of aggregate returns from a ward which is 75 per cent Jewish precludes a division of the population of Jews and, for example, Poles. It further precludes a subdivision of the Jews into rich Jews and poor Jews, German Jews and Russian Jews, etc. In short, while the use of such returns is admirable for charting the consistencies and shifts in the electoral behavior of the Jews since 1924, it is a rough instrument for attempting to explain the vote in any one year.

As may be seen from the footnotes in this chapter, considerable use was also made of the reported results of national sample surveys.

CHAPTER VI

An electoral decision is the product of many complex forces. To some extent it is the product of the influence which comes from involvement with primary groups, to some extent involvement with large demographic groups. What membership or involvement in such groups mean varies from individual to individual. These groups may overlap. For some voters, membership in such groups may not be perceived as relevant to electoral choice. Detective work may show otherwise.

In order to probe further the salient motivations of Jewish voters in a big city, a systematic sample of the eligible voters in Boston's Ward 14 were interviewed. A systematic sample simply means sampling at regular intervals from a prepared list. This method has also been called "quasi-random" (Mildred Parten, *Surveys, Polls, and Samples: Practical Procedures* [New York: Harper & Brothers, 1950]). Miss Parten describes the method used in this study (pp. 266-267), and also suggests that the method, if executed carefully enough, "seems close enough to random sampling" to permit the use of confidence limits which can be estimated for pure random samples.

THE SAMPLE DESIGN

Three hundred and fifty-one names were drawn from the Boston Police List, the first name drawn at random, the others at subsequent intervals of ten, excluding aliens and armed service members. After a total of 671 visits, 276 eligible voters in Ward 14 were interviewed. A total of seventy-five respondents (21 per cent of the sample) could not be interviewed for the following reasons: refused to be interviewed (nineteen); moved to unlocatable address (sixteen); moved out of Boston Metropolitan Area (fifteen); presented unmanageable problems of communication such as senility, language barrier, drunkenness, etc. (nine); respondent deceased (eight); respondent seriously ill (three); visited four times but not at home (four); reported missing by police and family (one).

Although the sample loss is about the same as sampling agencies experience when sampling with a list one year old, the rate of loss makes it difficult to know whether confidence limits can be applied to this survey at all. It is known that 75 per cent of the voters in the Ward cast their ballots for Stevenson. Yet, only 65 per cent of the voters in this sample acknowledged choosing the Democratic candidate. When a response to a question in a sample this size divides 65 per cent for and 35 per cent against, the chances are nineteen out of twenty that the true value of 65 per cent lies somewhere between 59 per cent and 71 per cent and the true value of 35 per cent is somewhere between 29 per cent and 41 per cent. Since the true value is known to be 75 per cent for and 25 per cent against Stevenson, there is a strong likelihood of sampling or reporting error. Chances are that the error derives from the fact that a certain percentage of voters forget who they voted for six months after the election, while still another proportion say they voted for the winner even when they did not. Nonetheless, the error in this case is small, and confidence may be placed in results which reveal gross tendencies.

THE INTERVIEW AND INTERVIEW SCHEDULE

The full interview took from twenty minutes to one-half hour with Jewish respondents, fifteen to twenty minutes with non-Jews. A total of thirty-five questions were asked. Some of these were broken down into subquestions, such as the ethno-religious involvement question, which included eighteen subquestions, or the question calling for an explanation of the vote, which included seventeen items. Indices were constructed for socioeconomic status, ethno-religious involvement, and political liberalism. It was decided that an elaborate SES scale would be too difficult to administer. Of the items considered for inclusion in the construction of the SES index—wealth, income, source of wealth and income, family history, occupational prestige—the only two chosen were occupational status and amount of income.

Occupational prestige was rated according to the seven-point scale recommended by W. Lloyd Warner (W. Lloyd Warner *et al., Social Classes in America* [Chicago: Science Research Associates, 1949], pp. 140-141), and adapted from the eleven-point scale used by Alba Edwards in the U. S. Bureau of Census. Scoring systems were worked out for constructing the EI and PL scales according to recommended statistical practices.

CHAPTERS 7, 8, 11

Bibliographical materials for these chapters may be found in the footnotes.

CHAPTERS 9, 10

Since the analysis of ticket splitting and minor party votes rests primarily on the appropriate use of aggregate election returns, the bibliographical and methodological notes for Chapter 5 apply here as well.

Index